WHEN YOU GET THERE

AN AUTOBIOGRAPHY

JENNIFER CARROLL

Advantage®

Shelton State Libraries
Shelton State Community College

Published by Advantage, Charleston, South Carolina.
Member of Advantage Media Group.

ADVANTAGE is a registered trademark and the Advantage colophon is a trademark of Advantage Media Group, Inc.

Printed in the United States of America.

ISBN: 978-159932-499-9
LCCN: 2014946037

Book design by George Stevens.
Cover photo by Richard Fleming.

This publication is designed to provide accurate and authoritative information in regard to the subject matter covered. It is sold with the understanding that the publisher is not engaged in rendering legal, accounting, or other professional services. If legal advice or other expert assistance is required, the services of a competent professional person should be sought.

Advantage Media Group is proud to be a part of the Tree Neutral® program. Tree Neutral offsets the number of trees consumed in the production and printing of this book by taking proactive steps such as planting trees in direct proportion to the number of trees used to print books. To learn more about Tree Neutral, please visit **www.treeneutral.com**. To learn more about Advantage's commitment to being a responsible steward of the environment, please visit **www.advantagefamily.com/green**

Advantage Media Group is a publisher of business, self-improvement, and professional development books and online learning. We help entrepreneurs, business leaders, and professionals share their Stories, Passion, and Knowledge to help others Learn & Grow. Do you have a manuscript or book idea that you would like us to consider for publishing? Please visit **advantagefamily.com** or call **1.866.775.1696.**

To my husband Nolan, thank you for all the years of unwavering love and support. To my children Nolan, Nyckie and Necho, you are the most amazing, loving, caring and devoted children and I am very proud of you all. I am grateful that God chose me to be your mother. I have the perfect family and I love you all more than words can express.

TABLE OF CONTENTS

INTRODUCTION

I n writing this book, I wanted to do two things. First, I wanted to give readers a sense of hope and some insight into how they can draw on their inner strength when faced with challenges by sharing with them some of the challenges I've been through in my own life. Second, I wanted to clear up inaccurate statements made about me in the media since I left my position as lieutenant governor of Florida in 2013. But this book's most important purpose is to motivate, inspire, and help others to overcome adversity, just as I've done in my own life.

I've had to overcome some big hurdles in my life, including coming to this country as an immigrant and assimilating into a different culture; fitting into a family that wasn't my biological family; serving in the male-dominated environment of the military; and going into politics and encountering a good-old-boy network. It wasn't easy, but my faith in the Lord and his provision of a strong family to lean on has helped me to move on from those hardships.

In the details I share in this book, I hope readers will see similarities with what they've been through, or are going through, in their own lives. Many people encounter situations that make them feel vulnerable, helpless, and withdrawn from life, like the ones I'll discuss in the coming pages. Such situations might cause sufferers to become extremely depressed, maybe even consider suicide.

When you're struggling, you never think you'll be better off because of it, particularly if you're a good person who's trying to do well. Bad things do happen to good people. You may blame yourself or second-guess the things you've done, but I believe God will always make a path through the storm. I believe you have to go through the storm to get to what's waiting on the other side and afterward, you'll be stronger. You'll be more capable of handling what comes. The pathway will be a little lighter, your vision a little clearer. That's when you may notice that what you thought was best for you wasn't the best thing after all. You learn to adjust and come out of these trying times stronger and more prepared for what's truly intended for you.

Part of what makes that possible is the people you surround yourself with. I have people who have been with me throughout all my difficulties, starting with my family.

My husband is a very reserved, quiet person, but he has stayed true to the core through all the ups and downs we've experienced together. He's not a political person or an extrovert who likes going out in public, but he's afforded me the flexibility to do the things that I enjoy doing, such as community service and civic engagement. He has a real sense of strength. Many men would feel their manhood threatened if their wives had a higher rank or pay than they had, but my husband was not concerned that he was an enlisted man and I was an officer. He's secure in who he is, which has brought me a sense of strength and helped me ascend to whatever levels I wanted to.

We also have three children who are my rocks. When I started in politics, the kids were young, but they always supported me during campaigns. I believe if you're involved in politics, you have to have your family's support all the way to be successful, because even with their support, political life can be hard. When you live in a fishbowl, with all your business out there for everyone to see (no matter whether your actions and words are portrayed truthfully or not), the family suffers as well. I've been very proud of my children for the way they've handled the difficult situations we've encountered. Their main concern has always been, "How is mommy feeling? Is she okay?" My husband takes the same approach. They've been a real source of strength and support.

They say that hard times show you who your real friends are, and that's been true for me. I'm not a person to socialize a lot, but I have made a number of acquaintances throughout the years who have supported me, prayed for me, or sent me scriptures to give me strength. Those who are for me outnumber those who are against me.

Many friends and family members gave me love and support. However, I want to give special acknowledgment to those who were immediately with me and gave me their support in my darkest hour. Psalms 55: 16–18 reads, "As for me, I will call upon God: and the Lord shall save me. He hath delivered my soul in peace from the battle that was against me: for there were many with me."

Thank you for your friendship.

Adeniyi Aderibigbe, Admiral Kevin Delaney (U.S. Navy Ret.), Alex Sivar, Althea Horne, Angela Thomas, Art and Jessica Rocker, Attorney John Fagan, the Baker family, Barbara Howard, Barney Spann, Bea Thomas, Beatriz Ramos, Becky and Brian Reichenberg, Bernice Pendry, Bert Williams, Beth Young, Bishop Ira Combs, Bishop Ron Dozier, Bob Sylvester, Brian Graham, Brian Swensen, Brian and Betsy Rupp, Captain Dave (U.S. Navy Ret.) and Sandy Faraldo, Caroline Wiles, Carolyn Kennedy, Charles and Candi Mecham, Charles Middleton, Chelsi Henry, Cheryl Basso, Chief Dana Shropshire (U.S. Navy Ret.), Chief David Perry, Chris and Kristin Seeger, Chris Enwasiki, Clarence McKee, Cliff Lee, Commissioner Barbara Stewart, Commissioner Chip Lamarka, Commissioner Phillip and Mrs. Cappie Walker, Commissioner Ronnie Robinson, Congressman David Rivera, Congressman J. C. Watts, Congressman Ted Yoho, Cynthia Miller (U.S. Navy Commander Ret.), Dale Landry NAACP President, Dana Shropshire (U.S. Navy Chief Ret.) and family, Daniel Jones, Danielle J. Ochoa, Daryl Barrs, David Dottin, David Griffin, David Hodges, Doug Darling, Dr. and Mrs. J. B. Williams, Dr. Eric Weise, Dr. Miya Burt-Stewart, Ed Wang, Ella Phillips, Elwyn Hall, Fabian Alzade, the Fletcher family, former city councilwoman Pat Locketfelder, former mayor Gow Fields, former representative Mike Weinstein, former representative Baxter Troutman, former representative Carlos Lopez Cantara, former representative Susan Goldstein, former representative Yolly Roberson, former representative Ralph Arza, former secretary of state Sandra Mortham, former senator Al Lawson, former senator Steve Wise, former senator Tony Hill, Frank and Ellen Pascellia, Frank N. James, General Buddy and Mrs. Gretchen Titshaw,

George Jakow, Gilda Opher, Glenn Joseph, Glo Smith and family, Gloria Fletcher and family, Godson Rashad Wentt, Gray Swoop, H. K. Matthews, Hank Rogers, Harry and Judy Burns, Harry Archon, Herschel Allen, Irma Guillory and family, Jan Glassman, Janice Galloway, Jean Morley, Jeff Camarda, Jim and Virginia Bumford, Joe Martory, Joseph Lewis , John and Felicia Davis, John and Mary Konkus, John Colon, John Hartmangruber (U.S. Navy Chief Ret.), Jorge Riano, Jose Bermudez, Judge Krista Marx, Judge Patt Maney, Judith Chapple, Judy Mount, Judy Rock, Karen Gornio, Keith and Earnestine Allen, Ken Ali, Kevin Chmielewski, Khoi Whittaker, Larry Wine, Leslie Dougher, Levi Williams, Lincoln Ford, Lisa Ard, Lori Ipar, Lourdes and Leo De La Pena, Lt. Governor Mead Treadwell, Lt. Governor Brian Krolicki , Lucas Gant, Lynette Meyers, Miriam Marlow, Marie McGee, Marili and Darryl Cancio, Marilyn and Bill Anatol, Marry Ann Carter, Mary Ellen and Bill Ludking, Matt Ubben, Mayor Gow Fields, Meridith Sanon, Michael Benjamin, Michael Monroe, Michael Long, Mike McCalister, Mike Weinstein, Millie Maldanado, Ming Chan, NAACP President Adora Ob Enwesi, NAACP President Isaha Rumblin, Naomi Roberts, Nancy Peek McGowan, Natalie Knight, Nicole Harshaw, Nita and Eddie B. Little, Pastor John E. Guns, Pastor Sam Pascoe, Pat and LouAnn McElvain, Pat Mooney, Patti Hartman, Phyllis Stephens, Prince Brown, Raynard Jackson, Renee Thompson, Representative Alan Williams, Representative Charles McBurney, Representative Charles VanZant, Representative Daryl Rouson, Representative Eddie Gonzales, Representative Hazelle Rogers, Representative Janet Atkins, Representative Matt Hudson, Representative Perry Thurston, Representative Ronald and Mrs. Tamara Renuart, Representative Will Weatherford, Richard Lee Scott, Rick Bebout,

Rob Jakubik , Robin Stublen, Rocky Cabral, Rogers Towers, Roy (U.S. Navy Chief Ret.) and Mrs. Diane Lyons, Ruth Stafford, Ryan Metzner, Sandy Aguilar, Sandra Owens, Scott Maddox, Sean Jackson, Secretary Terry Yonkers, Sel Buyuksarac , Selwyn Clarke, Senator Alan Hayes, Senator Arthenia Joyner, Senator Gary Siplen, Senator Steve Wise, Sharon Light, Sheela Van Hoose, Sheriff Will Snyder, Soror Cassandra Jenkins, Soror Cherry Alexander, Soror Edith and Frank Davidson, Soror Mamie Davis, Soror Nina Harley, State Attorney Angela Corey, Stephen and Shiela MacDonald, Steve Adams, Steven and Sheila Macdonald, Sue Cudjoe, Susie Wiles, Theo Jack, Theresa Jaipaul, Thomas and Barbara Miller, Tola Thompson, Tracy Dean, Valentina Williams, Van Royal, Vanessa Boyer, Vibert White, Wilie A. Miller, Yolanda Jackson.

JℒC

CHAPTER 1

AN ADOPTED CHILD

"Before I formed you in your
mother's womb, I chose you. Before
you were born, I set you apart."

—*Jeremiah 1:5*

I'm Trinidadian by birth and American by choice. When I was young, coming to America was a dream of many Trinidadians. America was seen as the land of plenty, and people would talk about all the great things they could achieve in America. As planes flew overhead, the children playing in the yard with me would look up and say, "Take me to America." Every plane we saw may not have been going to America, but we assumed it was. It was such a novelty to think that this land of enchantment actually existed. And then, when those who had left for America came back to visit, they were always decked out to the nines. They wore the latest clothes and jewelry. It seemed America was a place that had everything anybody could want.

What we didn't see was that some of those people were working two or three jobs as janitors or caretakers or some other kind of hard work that paid only modest wages. Some of them were using aliases and Social Security numbers that weren't theirs and running away from immigration. We didn't know any of that then. We just knew that America was the place to be.

America was the dream, but the reality was that my biological mother and father had difficulties. My father was an alcoholic, and when he drank, he was abusive. When I was three years old, my mother discovered that my father had had an affair with his secretary, who became pregnant. That was the last straw for her. She decided to move to America and make a different life for herself.

To do that, of course, she had to figure out what to do with her four children: me, an older sister, and a set of younger twin sisters. She had to put us somewhere until she could get herself together, so my siblings and I were left with my grandmother and grandfather. Subsequently, one of my twin sisters went to live with my mother's brother, and I ended up with my great aunt and uncle.

The story I was told, since I was only three and too young to remember, is that my mother and her sister would take me regularly to the home of their aunt and uncle, my great aunt and uncle, Jean and Carl Johnson. We were visiting them around the time my mother was looking to leave Trinidad, and when it came time to go, I said I didn't want to. I wanted to stay with my great aunt and uncle.

My great aunt and uncle loved the idea. They didn't have children of their own, so they agreed to watch me while my mother was gone. These were the people who became my parents. My biological mother, Yvonne, went off to the United States, where she attended nursing school and eventually remarried and had a new family. She came back a couple of times, but it never felt as if it were my mother coming back. She was just this stranger coming to visit. I do, however, thank her for choosing life and for bringing me into this world to be a blessing to my parents Carl and Jean.

People sometimes ask if it was hard being separated from my sisters and biological parents, but I was so young I don't remember much about that time. The hard part came later in life, when I reconnected with my biological mother and family in America. At that point, the friends of my adoptive mother, Jean, knew me only as her daughter, so it was almost taboo to talk about my other relations. In Jean's mind, I was hers. She was a bit jealous of my biological mother and afraid that I might go back to her. She always worried about that and, as a result, wanted to keep us separated.

But that would come later. At the time, I remember enjoying my life in Trinidad with my soon-to-be adoptive parents. In retrospect, it's a funny thing that so many people around me dreamed of going to America, because Trinidad was such a lovely country. We lived in a very good community. The music was great. The food was great. The people were friendly. You'll never meet a Trinidadian who's a stranger. Everybody is welcoming and inviting.

Trinidad gained its independence from the British Empire in 1962. It's a land of rich natural resources, including oil, pitch, liquid nitrate gas, agriculture, and fisheries. No one should ever go hungry in Trinidad, because everywhere you turn, there's some fruit tree or vegetable growing, even on the side of the road.

When I was growing up, crime wasn't much of anything either. Randolph Burroughs was the chief of police, and he was a tough nut. If you committed a crime, you might as well consider yourself dead or locked up for life. But if you were a good person,

My photo taken in Trinidad just before departing for America.

you really had no cares or worries. I've always wondered why America was so appealing to Trinidadians back then. I think it was just that when emigrants came back, they had all these new clothes and jewelry and their hair was well done. People still living on the island wanted those things too.

Life was good with my mother, Jean, and father, Carl. One thing about my parents is they always put me first. Whether it was my education, my upbringing, or the environment in which we lived, they were always thinking about how to make sure I would be successful. That's one of the reasons why they decided to emigrate to the United States. I couldn't go with them at first because I didn't have documentation under their name, so they went ahead to establish themselves before I went to live with them.

In Trinidad I lived with my parents on a big lot. There was a large house on the property where friends of my parents lived and a smaller mother-in-law house that my parents rented from them. Those friends, an older lady named Beebee and her husband, Mr. Clarke, took care of me while my parents went to the United States.

I was very sad when my parents left, but the Clarkes were nice and their children were my friends. Miss Beebee taught me how to clean. We had wood floors back then, which we had to mop, get down on all fours to put Simoniz wax on them, and then buffer them. I also did the washing and learned how to cook. I undertook these chores on a weekly basis.

One day, when I was about six years old, I walked to school by myself. I don't remember why I was walking alone on this particular day. The school was some distance from the house and I had to pass another school before I reached mine. As I did so, I encountered a man who asked me if I wanted to "f—k." It was the first time I'd ever heard that word, so I asked him what it meant. He said, "Come. Follow me."

We had outhouses back then. He lured me into one of them and whipped out his private part. It was the first time I'd ever seen a man's private part. It scared the mess out of me, and I didn't know what to do. First, I screamed, but there was no one to hear because everybody was already inside the school. Then, I slipped under his arm and pushed the door hard. I was able to get out, and I ran as fast as I could to school. Luckily, he still had his pants down, so he couldn't run after me.

I got away, but I was still petrified. I never told anyone about the incident because I felt it was my fault. I shouldn't have gone with him. I should have known better. After that, I was so scared I couldn't sleep and I never wanted to walk alone. I would beg somebody to walk with me to school.

I hope that anyone reading this story will make a point of listening to children when they have something sensitive to talk about. Don't make them feel embarrassed about what occurred, as if it were their fault. Take them at their word and investigate the situation. I hope the children in these situations will tell their parents what happened and not feel embarrassed about it, because, of course, they are not to blame. I think if my adoptive mother, Jean, hadn't been in America at the time, I probably would have told her, and she would have gone looking for the guy right away. But because there wasn't anyone I felt I could tell, I had to deal with it on my own.

After about a year and a half of separation, my father came back to get me. By then, it was a relief to leave Trinidad and be back under the cloak of my adoptive parents. They raised and took care of me. As an adult, I've been a big advocate for adoption because I'm so thankful for my adoptive parents. I think adoption is one of the greatest things you can do, one of the greatest loves you can provide. And adopted children shouldn't see themselves as outsiders. They should consider themselves special because their adoptive parents chose to include them in their family.

I know that my life would have turned out very differently if my parents hadn't chosen me, or actually, if we hadn't chosen each other, since I was the one who spoke up first and said I wanted to live with them. I just knew instinctively that they loved me. A child will pick up on that kind of love, even at a young age. I think I somehow knew that they offered a better environment than the broken-up situation my biological mother was leaving me in. Because my adoptive parents had no other kids in their home, I didn't have to compete with other children. It was just me.

After my father came to get me, we flew together to New York. I boarded the plane, decked out in my stockings and my nice dress, and I carried a baby doll that was as tall as I was. It was my first flight. The Pan Am stewardess said to me, "What are you going to do with your baby doll?" It was so big she put it in a compartment for the duration of the flight. When I saw how sharp those stewardesses looked, with their A-line skirts, neat jackets, and little caps, I decided right then that I wanted to be an airline stewardess. I thought it was the sharpest-looking thing I could do when I grew up.

The flight started off well, but my excitement didn't last. Back then, passengers were served a full plate of food—a real plate, with a real knife and fork and real food. It was a treat to be given this mountain of food, which included a nice chicken leg. I saved that chicken leg. It was going to be my feast of all feasts at the end of the meal. But before I could finish my food, I had to go to the bathroom. Lo and behold, when I came back, my plate was gone. They'd cleaned it up. I was always a respectful kid. I never spoke back to my parents, but I couldn't believe my father had let them take my chicken leg. I pouted for the rest of the flight.

We landed in New York and went to my parents' tiny apartment on Clarendon Road in Brooklyn. That was the start of a whole new life for me. I would reconnect with my biological mother down the road in America, but I never saw my biological father again. I'd hear about him from time to time, but that was all. He died in the 1970s in Trinidad of alcohol abuse. I remember hearing the news from my older sister and feeling empty because I'd never have an opportunity to know him.

I did a bit of soul searching after that, thinking about why the news made me feel so bad. It would have been nice to know if I looked like him or if we shared personality traits. But then I asked myself, "Could knowing these things have made my life any better?" The answer was no. I had great parents. I wanted for nothing. That was my solitude—that and recognizing that the life I had was what God intended for me. The parents he put in my path were the right ones for me. I didn't need to go looking for anything else.

As Dorothy discovered in *The Wizard of Oz*, which is one of my favorite stories, everything I needed was right there, all the time. That's what brought me peace of mind during that challenging time and during others I would face.

gsc

CHAPTER 2

AN IMMIGRANT
IN AMERICA

*"For God has not given us a
spirit of fear, but of power and
of love and of sound mind."*

—*2 Timothy 1:7*

rooklyn was so different from Trinidad. For one thing, we didn't have a yard. I can't remember how many stories our apartment building had, but it was tall. We had to use an elevator to get to our apartment, and there were all kinds of strangers living right on top of us. It was something I'd never seen before.

We had a one-bedroom apartment, so I slept on a bed that pulled out of an armchair in the living room. There was a ceramic panther that sat on a table in the room. That thing used to scare the bejeezus out of me at night. I would have nightmares that it was running after me.

My parents never shied away from a job. They both worked, often two or three jobs at a time. It was all to make sure they had enough to provide for me. My father worked as a janitor and mason at the Navy yard. He also worked as a pipe fitter and a dental technician and he would do odd jobs for people. He was very good with his hands and could make a number of repairs around the house, from plumbing to painting to carpentry. He even worked on cars. It was fascinating to be around my dad because he was a jack-of-all-trades. I liked to follow him around to see what he was doing (which I think led to my future career in aircraft maintenance for the Navy). Except for his work as a dental technician, for which he was trained at a U.S. school, he learned how to do all these things on the job.

I thought my mother's housework was boring. She cooked and ironed and cleaned. I didn't like that kind of thing at all, but since I was an only child, I had to help. I wasn't about to disrespect my parents. My mother was quick with the hand, but she was also a very proud and proper lady. She was always conscious of being a role model for me, someone I could emulate as I grew older. The lessons she taught me about caring for myself and being strong and independent followed me through my adult life.

My mother went to beauty school when she came to the United States. Then she earned a nurse's aide certificate. Much of her work when we were in Brooklyn was to provide in-home care for older and ailing people. One thing about my mother is she would not leave me with a babysitter. She took me with her when I wasn't in school, especially in the summertime. It was the worst because I had to stay in a room all day by myself until she finished her work. She didn't want the patients to know she had brought her child with her, so I had to stay really quiet—no TV, no radio, no talking. My mother would give me puzzles and *Dennis the Menace* books to read, but you can read only so much in a day. My mother would peep in every now and again, and if all were okay, she'd give me lunch and then go back to work.

I hated it, but I was always obedient because I knew my mother. It was just better to be quiet and do my part. Both my parents would get up around 4:00 a.m. to go to work, which meant I got up at 4:00 a.m. too, since I slept in the living room. We didn't have a car then, so we took public transportation everywhere. I always wanted to sleep, but that was a no-no. I was not allowed to sleep during the day, even when I was at my mother's workplace with nothing to do. I still had to do something constructive with my time—read a book, do homework, something.

Even on weekends, my parents would sleep no later than 6:00 a.m. Sundays meant church, so we got up early and were gone all day. We had to travel a distance to get to our Presbyterian Church. My father would sit on the outside of the pew, and I would be in between my parents. He always fell asleep, but if I ever nodded off, I got a pinch from my mother.

After the church service, we didn't just go home. We spent time with Pastor Oliver. Then, we'd visit the attorney who had helped my parents organize their paperwork to become citizens and formally adopt me. His office was just a block away, so we'd go there to socialize. That was another time when I had to sit and be quiet. Children were to be seen and not heard. I had to wait until they finished before we could go home and enjoy our weekly Sunday feast.

My mother would start cooking on Saturday. She always cooked a big meal even though only the three of us would eat it, because "If anybody should stop by, at least we'll have enough food." Not that many people stopped by. She made dishes such as macaroni and cheese, which we call macaroni pie in Trinidad, and Trinidadian dishes such as stewed meat and callaloo. And we always had dessert—pound cake and fruitcake. My father was a small man—5'6" tall and about 165 pounds in weight—but he never gained weight despite all the food my mother made from scratch.

Weekdays revolved around school, of course. My school was just down the street from our apartment. I'd walk to school each day, and that was scary for me. It brought back bad memories from Trinidad. School was scary too. It was different because I spoke with a West Indian accent, and the other children teased me for it. "Why are you talking so funny?" they'd ask. "What's wrong with you?"

I learned to be very quiet. I didn't have friends because my parents were so strict. The rule was if I had any friends, my parents had to meet their parents, had to know where they lived, and had to have their phone number. I thought all that was so cumbersome that I didn't bother. I didn't tell my parents that, but that's what I thought. I never talked back to my parents. Never.

In school I was a loner. I didn't take kindly to the teasing, so I figured I might as well stay by myself. I thought I'd stay out of trouble that way, too. That didn't pan out, because the bullies spotted me in a heartbeat. Some girl would say something such as "You think you're too good for us?" And then she'd want to fight. Twice I got into a fight in elementary school. The first time, I didn't fight back. I went home crying and my father asked me what happened. I told him and he said, "You didn't defend yourself?"

"I didn't want to get in trouble," I told him. I thought that was the right answer, but his response was, "Now you're going to get in trouble with me because you didn't defend yourself."

After that, his instruction to me was "I'm not sending you to school to get into any fights. You don't start anything, but if something gets started, you better finish it. Otherwise, you are going to get a beating from me as well." That opened the door for me to defend myself. The same girl challenged me again, and I stood up for myself that time. I didn't really know how to fight, so I just went in swinging. I was the victor, and that was the last time I was bullied by her.

The social part of school may have been difficult, but once I was in class, everything was fine. My studies weren't hard for me at all because schooling in Trinidad was so good then (and still is—Trinidad has a 98 percent literacy rate). When I was young, the results of tests, which everyone took, were practically plastered in the sky. They showed everybody who had passed and who had failed, so nobody wanted to fail. There was such an emphasis on education that students who came to the United States often jumped grades. In fact, my teacher called my mother in to discuss whether I should skip a grade. My mother asked me about it, and I said I preferred to stay where I was. Although the environment I was in was difficult, I was worried that the older kids might be even worse.

At home my parents made sure I studied. My father was the one who reviewed my homework because he had more patience than my mother. If my mother tried to explain something to me and I wasn't getting it, she would hit me on the head. My father was a little better. He would break things down for me. Every night they reviewed my homework to make sure it was done correctly and that I understood all the information. So I always got good grades, and my behavior marks were even better. All my teachers would say, "She is absolutely wonderful. An outstanding student. Doesn't talk much. We wish we could duplicate her." My mother would come back and say, "Now who is that child they're talking about?" But my parents loved getting those reports.

When I was a child, my fun usually revolved around my parents, particularly my father. If my parents went to dinner, to a friend's house, or on a trip, I was always included. My father loved to play musical instruments. He played the saxophone and the clarinet. He wanted me to play one too, so I chose the clarinet, but I could never get a sound out of the darn thing. He hired a music tutor for me, but I hated the vibration of the wood on my lips. I continued with it because he wanted me to, but I was never good at it. As a matter of fact, after my parents passed away, I found that clarinet in their house and I donated it.

There really wasn't much time for fun back then, and definitely not enough time to get into trouble. My parents, particularly my mother, always seemed to know where I was and what I was doing at all times.

My mother used to tell me that if I didn't behave, she would send me back to Trinidad. When I was young, I believed her. It was very frightening. Looking back, I know she never would have done it because I was her life. She said it to keep me on the straight and narrow.

She was dealing with her own fears too. I didn't really understand that until much later, but she was being fed whispers from my father's sister and others who said, "She's not your child. She's going to find her biological mother and forget about you one day. All of what you're doing for her is going to be for naught." Who knows why they said a thing like that. It wasn't true, but I think that thought was always in my mother's head.

Then, of course, since I was a girl, she wanted to make sure I stayed away from boys and didn't do whatever she thought other kids were doing. I was always thinking, "I don't want to do anything wrong because I don't want to go back to Trinidad. There's nobody there for me. Who would take care of me? What would I do?" I envisioned myself being there all alone in the dirt with no one to take care of me, no home to live in, no food to eat, no clothes to wear. It was a frightful vision. Fear kept me out of trouble.

All the while, the fact that I was adopted wasn't really talked about. It wasn't until my biological mother, Yvonne, wanted to have a connection with me that I really understood the situation. Yvonne had her own family by then, and she didn't want to take me away, but she did want to see me. She didn't push it, because she wanted to be mindful of her aunt's feelings. It wasn't until I was a teenager that I was able to visit her and her family. They were living close by, in Queens, New York, and my parents would take me for short visits, maybe 20 minutes to an hour. I didn't have enough time to develop any sort of relationship with her or my siblings. And it wasn't something my mother and I talked about, either. It was something that just kind of happened. I knew this woman we were visiting was my biological mother, but I had to suppress whatever feelings I had about that. I worried about hugging Yvonne for too long or showing her too much affection. I was always concerned about not hurting my adoptive mother's feelings.

It was a tough thing to go through, but it also taught me something that I've carried with me throughout my entire life, which is how to have empathy for others. Sometimes, that's been a negative, when my empathy has overridden my own sense of self-preservation. But usually, it's a positive. I loved, respected, and appreciated my parents so much that I never wanted them to regret choosing me as their child.

I can't really blame my mother for being afraid, or my parents for being so strict. They always looked out for my best interests. As I grew older, they saw that it was time for us to have more space (I couldn't keep sleeping on that chair in the living room, after all). They also wanted a better school for me, so they started looking for a house. That's when we moved to Wyona Street in Brooklyn. It was the first home they'd purchased. It was a two-story house with a basement and a small backyard. We lived on the first floor, which had a full kitchen, a dining area, a living room, a formal dining room, two bedrooms, and bathrooms. The basement was ours too, but the upper floor had two separate apartments, which they rented out.

We moved there when I was in upper elementary school. My elementary school was just a block away, and my junior high school was a couple of blocks across the main road. I was a latchkey kid when I was in junior high since both my parents worked. I had to make sure I called my mother the moment I got home from school each day. She had timed how long it should take from school to home without stopping. If I was late or didn't call the minute I got home, I was in trouble. Once I got home, I would find a list of tasks to keep me occupied. I had to start preparing dinner by peeling this or boiling that. She left clothes for me to iron, such as her work uniform, my father's pj's, even towels and sheets.

I also had to do my homework and take care of the dog. My dad was always picking up strays. The backyard was small, so the dog was left inside all day. When I got home, I had to clean up the mess, mop the floor, and then feed the dog. We usually had only one at a time, but we always had one. If a dog left or died, my father would find another one somewhere. He was an animal lover. Sometimes he'd trap birds too, and I had to clean their cage. Sometimes, we had fish in a bowl I had to clean. I was the animals' janitor.

All this was my parents' way of filling my time so I didn't get into trouble. If the work wasn't done, my mother would notice when she got home and I'd have to explain what I'd been doing. I figured it was just simpler to do the work. Ms. Goldstein, who lived in one of the apartments, kept an eye on me. If I left the house or if anybody came over, she would tell my mother. I knew Ms. Goldstein was always watching, so I wasn't about to do anything wrong. It was as if I had all these bricks over my head that kept my feet on solid ground.

It worked too. I never rebelled. I never talked back. However, I did get into trouble for things I *didn't* do. For example, across the street from the elementary school was a corner store. The shopkeeper sold French fries for five cents a bag and there was a jukebox, so a lot of kids stopped in there after school. Again, I wasn't very friendly with other kids, but I would sometimes peek in on my way home just to see what new dances they were doing. Then I'd come home and practice by myself so if I ever happened to go out with my parents someplace where people were dancing, I'd know what to do. One day, somebody told my mother I had been dancing in the corner store. My mother should have known that I was too quiet to be dancing with other kids. Plus, she clocked when I arrived home from school. So it should have been obvious I hadn't had enough time to dance at the store. It clearly wasn't me this person had seen, but if anybody told my mother I had done something bad, that was gospel, and I was punished for it. I got a belt whipping for dancing in the corner store. I was very upset to be whipped for something I hadn't done.

I remember getting into trouble only once for something that was my fault. It was when Aunt Daisy, one of my father's sisters (he had nine brothers and sisters), and her family moved from England to New York. They needed a place to live, so my father fixed up the basement for them to stay in until they got themselves together. Aunt Daisy had two boys. The three of us were playing one day when one of them shoved the other into the wall, leaving a hole. It was right at the entranceway to the basement, so my father saw it as soon as he came home. He asked me what had happened, but the boys and I had agreed we weren't going to say anything. I was protecting them, but when I told my father I didn't know, he said, "You've been home and you don't know what happened? The wall is not going to get a hole by itself. Something happened."

So he pulled aside one of the boys, who spilled his guts. That was the first beating I ever received from my father. My mother was the one who carried out all the beatings before that. My father said that this was my house, and I should have been protecting it. He said this ought to be a lesson not to lie and cover up for somebody. I have never lied for anyone since.

While he was whipping me, the belt slipped and the buckle cut my thigh. It wasn't a deep cut. Still, my father felt very bad about it. He never beat me after that, but I still have that scar to remind me.

My parents were strict, but it's not as if they had no reason to worry. I remember an incident with my father that shook them both to the core. He had been working two jobs and was able to save up enough money to buy an eight-millimeter movie camera. He was so proud of himself because he would be able to make home movies of our family. My dad took public transportation to work, and he was robbed when coming home on the train. The robbers took my father's salary, because he'd cashed his paycheck that day, and they also took the items he had bought, including the camera.

My mother was worried even before he arrived home, because he was pretty regular about his schedule and that night he was later than usual. The look on his face when he walked in the door was as if his whole life was gone, as if someone had just invaded his space and his family and he was powerless to do anything about it. It was almost as if he was embarrassed to come home to his family empty-handed. I remember that look to this day. I always thought of my father as a very strong man, but that was one of his weakest moments that I ever saw. Because he was my dad, it was heart wrenching to see him like that.

The robbery was a real eye-opener, a wake-up call about the ills of society and how they can plague any family at any time. It was the first time my father had had anything stolen from him. For me, it meant an additional layer of protection from my parents, to the point where I couldn't go anywhere without them, even though I was in junior high by then. Meanwhile, my father went out and did odd jobs to make up for the money he'd lost, because he still had bills to pay.

Around the same time, an incident occurred in our home that involved me. My parents were entertaining some friends for dinner, and I was in the kitchen washing up when one of my father's friends came in. Our house had a long corridor between the living room and the kitchen, so I was a distance from where the adults were at the time. My father's friend was a tall man, about 6'1". He put his hands on the counter on both sides of me, locking me into the area by the sink. Then he propositioned me. I was scared to no end. Luckily, just as I had done back in Trinidad, I was able to dodge underneath his arm and run into my room. I didn't tell my parents because I didn't know how to explain that their friend had done this in their home while they were right down the hall. I also thought if I did tell them, my dad would get into a fight that might cause him trouble.

Luckily, even though I never said anything, that man never came back to our house. I don't know why—maybe he was afraid I had told my parents—but whatever the reason, it was a relief never to see him again. That incident, and the one in Trinidad, made me very aware of how vulnerable young girls are to predators. It's a difficult situation for a young woman, and feeling comfortable enough to speak out about such things is something adults have to encourage. The best thing any child can do is to speak up, regardless of whether it's going to bring tension. At least that child has spoken out and somebody knows the situation occurred. Looking back, I wish I had told my parents about both encounters.

In my second year of junior high, we moved again. Gang activity was flaring up in Brooklyn at the time, and the neighborhood was getting a little rough. My parents, as always, were concerned about providing a safe environment for me, so they decided to purchase a home in Hempstead, Long Island. That's where we lived until I left home as an adult. It was a bigger home and my father had a car. Of course, a bigger house meant I had more chores to do.

I had my first date around that time. I was not allowed to date, but the junior prom was coming up and I wanted to go. A young man in my class, named Peter, asked me to go to the prom with him. I told him I would, but I'd have to meet him there so my parents wouldn't know. Of course, if I went anywhere, my parents drove me. So, on the night of the prom, they dropped me off at 8:59 p.m. (the prom started at 9:00 p.m.) and two hours later, when it was scheduled to end, they were there to pick me up, right on the dot.

Of course, no one else got to the prom on time, so things didn't really get going until about the time I had to leave. Here's this young man thinking we're on a date and, all of a sudden, I turn to him and say, "I've got to go. My parents are here to pick me up." That just ruined everything.

It was a similar situation when I went to my high school senior prom. I still wasn't allowed to date, although I snuck around and saw a young man named Oliver. My mother actually encouraged me to go to the prom. Oliver's family and mine were friendly, so she approved of him as my date, thinking I was just going with a family friend, not someone I especially liked.

My dad, on the other hand, was mad that my mother had encouraged me. When I was all dressed up and ready to go, my mother was there, her friends were there, and my godparents were there, but my father was nowhere to be found. He was off pouting somewhere. My mother suggested I wait a little while before leaving, so I did. Oliver and I were finally about to go when my dad pulled up in his car. I said, "Dad, I'm leaving," and he just gave me a grunt.

My mother told me to be back by 11:00 p.m., which made me nervous from the start because the prom was all the way in New York City. It didn't start until 9:00 p.m. and it would take time to drive all the way back to Long Island. So I was late coming back. I was so worried about it that my stomach was upset all the way home. I thought my parents were going to kill me that night.

I arrived home about a half hour late, and wouldn't you know, both my parents were sleeping. They hadn't even noticed. I had dodged a bullet.

I loved my parents and I so appreciated them, although, sometimes, I thought their rules were unfair. Now, as a mother of three, I put myself in their position. I'm not as tough on my kids as my parents were on me (although my kids may think differently), but my kids have grown up in a very different environment. My parents were dealing with all this uncertainty about having a child, particularly a girl who wasn't theirs by birth, about being older parents, and about raising a child in America, which was such a different environment from Trinidad. Looking back, I can understand why they did what they did. And in the world of politics, it worked out in my favor. If my parents hadn't been as strict as they were, if I'd been a loose goose with boyfriends all over the place, people would have been able to say that I wasn't a prim and proper girl. Each of us has our paths to follow. One may seem better than another, but what's for you is for you. You just have to deal with it and move forward. As my parents grew older and I had to take care of them, I saw how much they appreciated and loved me. The depth of love that they had for me was unbelievable.

$\mathcal{G\&C}$

CHAPTER 3

BALANCING ACT 1:
A WOMAN IN
MILITARY LIFE

"For I know the plans I have for you,
'declares the LORD,' plans to prosper
you and not to harm you, plans to
give you hope and a future."

—*Jeremiah 29:11–12*

Joining the military was all about being able to leave home in a respectful way. When I graduated from high school I wanted to be independent, I wanted space to breathe, but I didn't want my parents to feel I didn't appreciate them. That meant finding employment so I could take care of myself and a career path that I could do something with, but it wasn't my idea to join the Navy. As I said before, when I first came to the United States, I had it in my head that I wanted to become an airline stewardess because that uniform was so doggone sharp.

My mother had initially said I could go away to college, but then, after I'd been accepted at all these places, she changed her mind. "No, you can't go *away* to college," she said. "You have to go to college here." That meant living at home for another four years. I thought, "Oh my God, I'll never get out of here."

Then a family friend suggested I look into joining the Navy, as he had. However, he recommended that I go in as an officer, not as an enlisted person, which is what he'd done. But he didn't really explain how it all worked. I was just coming out of high school and didn't have a degree, and I didn't realize that to join as an officer, you had to either go into the Navy's ROTC program to earn a degree or already have a degree. I also didn't understand that there was a difference between an officer recruiter and an enlisted recruiter, so I went to the enlisted recruiter and asked him about the officer program. He told me, "Oh, it's better to come into the enlisted ranks because you will get more training and experience." What he didn't tell me was he had a quota. He had to sign up a certain number of people, and if he'd sent me over to the officer recruiter, that recruiter would have gotten the points. So he convinced me it was better to join the enlisted ranks.

At the time, my green card was being finalized under the name of Johnson, my adoptive parents' name. I had my documentation, but not the actual green card that the military needed, so I had to go through a lawyer to get it. That delayed my departure for active duty. I stayed in the delayed entry program for about six months, waiting for completion of my paperwork and working as a volunteer in the recruitment office to keep myself busy.

Another reason I chose the Navy was because, when I walked down the hall where all the military recruiters were, the Air Force's door was closed. I didn't want to have anything to do with mud or anything messy like that, so the Army was out. The Marines were just a bunch of guys, and I didn't want to be a burly girl. But the Navy had these salt-and-pepper uniforms that were sharp—white shirt and black pants with a garrison cap. That's why I gravitated toward the Navy. It was the uniform. It wasn't quite like that stewardess's uniform I'd seen when I came to the United States, but in my dress uniform—oh yeah—I looked sharp.

What a way to decide your future. What was I thinking? But joining the Navy did give me the chance I wanted to flex my wings. My dad didn't like the idea at all. He wanted me to stay at home and go to school, which is what I ended up doing for a time while waiting for my paperwork. I went to Nassau Community College and took a few classes. Those credits gave me a leg up when I finally entered the military. I didn't have to start my education from scratch, so I was able to finish my associate's degree pretty quickly while stationed in Hawaii.

My father blamed my mother for giving me permission to join the military. I was 18 years old and could do what I pleased, of course, but to be respectful, I asked them first. My mother said okay, but my dad said, "What does she have to go away for?" He didn't have a plan for what I should do instead; he just didn't want me to go. I think he wanted to be able to protect me forever.

Eventually, my papers came through, and in 1979 I went off to boot camp in Orlando, Florida. That was the first time I'd left home on my own. Except for one trip with my mother to Venezuela and Trinidad, I'd barely been out of the state since we'd come to the United States. Besides that, the only thing I knew about the military was what I'd seen on *Gomer Pyle*. So with no idea of what I was getting myself into, I boarded a plane to Orlando.

When I arrived, it was the dark of night. I was hauled onto this battleship-gray bus that looked like something that would transport prisoners. I sat with all these other recruits who came in at the same time, and that's when the yelling started. Some recruits thought they knew what the military was all about and they boasted that their friend, or cousin, or whoever, had told them what to expect. Those were the ones who'd get us into the most trouble in the days to come. They'd open their big mouths and we'd all end up doing pushups or extra marching or something.

The bus passengers were all women. Orlando was the only boot camp, at the time, where men and women were trained on the same compound but were still separated. The men couldn't watch the women and the women couldn't watch the men. Fraternization was not allowed.

We arrived at boot camp, where petty officers started yelling orders at us. They took our civilian clothes away and gave us uniforms. They assigned us bunks and told us exactly how we were supposed to fold our sheets. They assigned chores to everybody. I was put in charge of laundry detail. We didn't sleep the whole night because we had to go through all these preliminaries. Everything was completely different from what I was used to. First of all, I had not shared a room with anyone for quite a while. Here I was, having to share a dorm with a whole bunch of strangers. And I was assigned a top bunk, which I hated. I'd never slept on a double-decker bed before.

I didn't talk much, and I think that came in handy. Instead, I observed a lot. At that time, I didn't have an outgoing personality because of how I'd been brought up. Instead, I thought of my time there as a business. I was there to do a job. I had eight weeks of training to go through before my military career would begin.

It wasn't exactly a fun experience, but I got through it. One day I was assigned duty on the *Union Jack*, a ship docked at the base. I was sent there because I'd just had four wisdom teeth extracted. I think the military's way of training dentists was to let them practice on recruits, because almost all those who came through boot camp had their wisdom teeth taken out.

Since I couldn't do any strenuous exercises or marching for a few days, they gave me light duty on the *Union Jack*. One morning, the chief petty officer onboard asked me if I would like to raise the flag. I thought that was such a great honor. I was very touched to even be asked. I went through the ritual of marching while holding the flag (all the while scared to death I would drop it), latching it onto the lanyard, and hoisting it up as the trumpet sounded. In that moment, I really felt awestruck and connected with this country. Even to this day, I get goose pimples when I think about it.

I made it through my eight weeks of training, not realizing how much they actually held our hands during that time. They picked us up at the airport and transported us to the base. They gave us everything we needed and told us what to do. Everything was controlled. But then, when we graduated from boot camp, we were on our own.

First, I went home to visit my parents, which was boring. All the old restrictions were still in place, so I was ready to leave when the time came. But all the Navy did at that point was give recruits a plane ticket to travel to their command. After boot camp, most recruits went to an "A" school, which is where they received training for the rate, or job, that they were going to do. The "A" schools are located in various places throughout the United States. My "A" school would have been in Memphis, Tennessee, where they trained jet mechanics, if I had gone that route. However, I entered the Navy as a non-rate airman recruit, knowing only that I was going to do something in the aviation field. My recruiter had tried to persuade me to go into one of the fields in which the Navy usually placed women, such as administrative work or nursing. But since I'd always loved working with my dad on mechanical, plumbing, masonry, or painting projects, I wanted to do something like that, not any of the so-called girl jobs.

Aviation appealed to me, based on what I read in the Navy's book of job descriptions, but I wasn't assigned to a particular area. Aviation maintenance comprises a number of different areas. You could choose to work as a mechanic, an avionics technician, an airframes technician, and so on. At the time, they hadn't opened up much of the aviation field to women. However, it just so happened that when I came out of boot camp, they were starting to allow women to work as jet mechanics.

So there I was, headed for my command. I had actually left early to escape my parents' rules and boarded a plane to Hawaii. It didn't dawn on me until I landed that I had no idea what I was supposed to do when I got there. "Wait a minute," I thought. "They are not going to pick me up as they did before. Who am I going to call? Where is the base? How am I going to get there?"

It was 10 at night. Luckily, when I walked into the terminal, I saw someone in a Navy uniform and I asked, "I need to go to Barbers Point, but I don't know where it is or how to get there. Is there transportation that goes there?"

He said no, there was no transport. So then, I really started to worry. He asked which command I was checking into and I told him I didn't know. So he asked to see my orders, and I showed them to him. He was the duty officer driver at Pearl Harbor, which is in the opposite direction to Barbers Point, but finally he said, "I'll get in trouble if I go out of my way, but if you don't tell anybody, I'll take you out there."

He was willing to trust me and I had to trust him too, because he could have taken me out to the pineapple fields for all I knew. But he drove me all the way to Barbers Point and dropped me off at the duty office. I checked into the barracks and, the next day, checked into my command. I was telling my command master chief the story of how I'd arrived when he looked at me and asked, "What's this petty officer's name? We'd like to call his command and send him an appreciation letter." But the guy had told me not to tell anyone or he'd get in trouble, so I said, "I did not commit his name to memory."

In my new command, I worked on the line, which is where the grunt work occurs. I was sweeping bird poop out of hangar decks, fueling aircraft, and washing them with Turco solution, which can blind you or burn your skin. My line chief was an aviation jet mechanic. Each week the whole command would lock down to do professional training, and when my line chief went to the mech shop to train the mechanics, I would follow him because I thought what he was doing was interesting. That's what moved me toward getting my designation as a jet mechanic. I loved learning about combustion, engines, and all the mechanics that allowed the plane to fly.

I was learning a lot on the job, and I was learning a lot about living life on my own, as well. I had my own apartment in a little townhouse and was living on a budget, or rather, the lack thereof. I didn't have much furniture, so cardboard boxes served as my tables, dresser, and desk. I had a bed, but that was about it. Still, I got this idea that I wanted to purchase my first car.

I was 19 years old, and like a lot of young people starting out, I felt the salary I was making was mine to spend. Instead of looking for a practical car that would still leave me with some resources at the end of the month, I decided to get a Nissan 280 ZX.

I didn't understand that I needed credit to buy something like that. I'd never had a credit card or a loan before. A nice fellow at work, named Tony, had established credit for himself and he took a liking to me. He decided he would cosign for me so I could get credit cards and qualify for a loan to buy furniture. Looking back, that was really trusting of him since he didn't know me well. After all, I had just arrived at the command. But thanks to Tony, I was able to establish my credit and take out a loan for that 280 ZX.

I did everything I needed to do to make sure I got the car I really wanted. The problem was that between paying my rent, electricity, insurance, and the car loan, I was using up every penny I made. At the end of the month, all I had left was $24 to my name, never mind any entertainment, gas, food, or savings. It hit me like a brick one day. Why am I stuck with this car and having next to nothing to my name at the end of the month?

I was determined not to ask my parents for anything. My dad had given me an allowance when I lived at home and he would have still contributed if I needed it, but I didn't want that. I thought, "I'm a big girl. I'm out on my own and I don't need to rely on my parents to take care of me anymore. They did enough while I was growing up."

Fortunately, the dealer bought the car back from me. I traded it in for a used Nissan B210, which served me very well through

As a plane captain I took ownership and pride in my planes taking off and coming back safely.

Out of the hundreds of sailors in my command, I was honored to be selected Sailor of the Quarter.

Being a mustang gave me a level of respect and loyalty from all of my enlisted shipmates that is rarely seen in the civilian work environment.

I was elated to see my family after a long six months deployment overseas.

all the years I was in Hawaii. That was a wake-up call and a lesson in financial literacy 101. I didn't take money for granted after that, and just as my parents had once done, I picked up additional jobs to earn some extra money. Over the years, I did everything from delivering telephone books door-to-door, to working as a cashier at a grocery store, to being a receptionist for AMF bowling. I even did a bit of modeling work for commercials and magazine ads.

While working full-time and picking up odd jobs, I also went to school to earn my associate's degree, and I studied on my own for the Navy's exams, because the only way to advance in rank was to pass exams. And even if you passed, you were still competing with thousands of Navy personnel nationwide who were applying for the same rank. There were only so many slots, so not everybody who passed would advance in rank. To compete, you had to get better than good-enough grades and have great evaluations.

Every test I took, I passed and advanced. I also received awards, such as Sailor of the Quarter and Airman of the Quarter. As a young E-3, I was given the position of line shift supervisor at night. That didn't go over well with some of my male counterparts. I was working mostly with men at that point. Since aviation was a new field for women, there were very few of us. For most of my commands, I was either the only woman, or one of two or three women, or the only black woman officer. When I left the Navy, there were more women coming into the field because restrictions had been lifted in all areas except nuclear ships and submarines, which women still can't serve on.

It was during that time that I had my first encounter with inappropriate sexual remarks in the work place and racism. That may sound surprising, but I'd never experienced it before, maybe because of the protective cloak that my parents had me under. But when I became a line shift supervisor, the name-calling started. I was the "black—" (expletive). There was a lot of animosity, not only because I was a woman in what many thought was a man's world, but also because I had a lower rank than some of them, so they didn't think I should have the position.

One night, one of the petty officers, who resented the fact that he hadn't been given the position of line shift supervisor, was leaving the island to transfer to a new duty station. The night shift was supposed to last from 3:00 to 11:00 p.m., but if the planes weren't ready for missions the next day, we might work until 7:00 a.m. when the next shift came in or whenever the maintenance chief said we could go. On this particular night, one of the planes was giving us a lot of trouble. Operations needed the plane to fly the next day, so the entire shift should have been working through the night. But since this petty officer was departing the next day and because he was being a pain in the neck, I let him go early.

But that wasn't enough for him. Two women, who were his friends, worked in the line shack. He wanted them to party with him as he twilighted out, so they asked me if they could go too. I said, "No. We have work to do, and I'm not going to stay here and do it by myself while you guys go party." When they told him they couldn't go, he called me all kinds of racial names.

He was off work at the time, but the line was right next to a dirt lot where we parked our cars. He was standing by his vehicle, near the airplane we were working on, when he said these things, so the other people there heard him. This incident gave me good training in keeping my composure. I could have yelled and cussed back at him, but I kept my cool, probably because I was so stunned. This was new territory for me.

I really wasn't sure how to handle it, so I went back to the line check and I prayed, "Lord, help me deal with this." Then I went into maintenance control and told the maintenance chief petty officer that I had let this guy go early, but he was still harassing me and calling me names. That's all I did. I didn't respond to the guy at all. We worked the rest of the night, and he went on his way. But the next morning, the maintenance chief told my line division chief what had happened. By the time I came into work, he already knew. My division chief then went to the command master chief and told him what had happened. The command master chief took it to the commanding officer, who was Commander Curtis. And the guy was brought up on captain's mast, which means he was reduced in rank and fined before he even got to his new duty station. Then the command master chief said to me, "You do not mess with my crème de la crème."

I'd never heard those words before, so I said, "What does that mean?" He said, "It means you're the cream of the crop. You're one of my best airmen. I can rely on you. You don't get into trouble. You do everything you're told, and that guy is not going to get away with this." I had no idea they thought so highly of me until that moment.

That action sent shock waves throughout the command. It let folks know that behavior like that wasn't going to be tolerated. That was important because changes were taking place. The Navy was no longer exclusively a man's world. We were starting to have women in the Navy workshops to address sexism. Some of the chief petty officers, who had been there for years, had never had to work with women before. And they didn't want to. They thought women were going to use excuses such as pregnancy and doctor's appointments to not tow their weight. They were very opposed to women being in *their Navy*, as they used to call it, and they were not shy to show their disapproval.

These men didn't want to admit that women brought attributes and experience to the job that could be useful. For example, sometimes we'd have to go into some of the buddy stores, which are external tanks that attach to the wing of an aircraft for the purpose of refueling, or we'd have to change the seals, and so on. Most of the men had hands that were too big to fit inside some of the machinery. My little hand was able to get right in and do what the men couldn't do.

We also had the A-4 aircraft, a single engine with the fuselage attached from front to back. If we had to do any work on the aircraft without pulling apart the fore and aft, it took smaller hands to get inside to turn a wrench or do wiring. Having women working on those planes reduced the time it took to finish the job.

We brought a different flavor to the job that could be really positive, so why, I wondered, were these men so reluctant to have us there? This fight against women colleagues went on for a number of years, but eventually, a lot of the old guard left the Navy, either because it was their time to retire or because they didn't like the way things had changed. I always hoped that having women around would just become the norm after a while, because as the generations cycled through, that would be the only thing the younger men knew. But I realized after a while that more needed to happen for significant changes to take hold. The chief petty officers really ran the Navy, and their knowledge was imparted to the younger generation, along with, it seemed to me, some of their bad habits and old ways of thinking. The cycle had to be broken.

I was able to break the cycle, at least in my command, when I became an officer. In that command, we'd go away on six-month deployments, which meant we had to pack up the entire squadron, including all our airplanes, and go overseas for six months. Back then, we didn't have Skype or e-mail to keep in touch with our friends and families. If we wanted to communicate with someone back home, it usually meant paying $100 for a 10-minute phone call or writing a letter—snail mail, as we used to call it—which could take months to arrive. Some of the male senior chief petty officers believed women were purposely becoming pregnant to get out of going on deployment, because pregnancy was one of the restrictions. If you were pregnant, you couldn't go. Instead, you'd go to another command and do light duty until you had the baby.

One day, when I was a maintenance officer, one of my best workers on the line, a young woman, was crying. I asked her what was wrong, and she said she had just found out she was pregnant. "So why are you crying?" I asked her. "This should be a joyous moment." She said, "The maintenance master chief is going to accuse me of getting pregnant to get out of going on deployment, and I can't face that."

That was a ball that hit me in the head. I now had a rank that allowed me to speak up for these young women who were my juniors and afraid to speak up for themselves. After all, if a man had just found out his wife or girlfriend was going to have a baby, he would be ecstatic. Why couldn't this young woman be just as excited about the life she was creating?

I knew I had to get up the nerve to say something, but that meant confronting the master chief. The master chiefs were really rough. They would cuss at anything that moved. They used the f-bomb all the time, f-ing this and f-ing that, until I finally said, "Listen, you don't use that language around your wife or mother. You wouldn't want it used around your children. So do not use it in my presence or around the people who work for me. If you want to say something, say fudge." After that, I had all these grown men going around saying "fudging" this and "fudging" that.

The master chief was big, about 6'. He had already been through a divorce, and he didn't think too highly of women at that particular time because his wife had taken him to the cleaner's, or so he said. But I walked up to him. "Master Chief, I need to speak with you."

I told him the situation with the young woman. "First of all, even if you feel she's making excuses, you're not going to say so. Second, when you look at the statistics, the men have taken more time off for their basketball injuries and back or knee problems from recreational stuff than our women have taken off for maternity or anything else. So don't judge these women or make them feel they've done something terribly wrong. If you had a family, you would be happy if your wife told you she was having a baby. So, our women should be able to feel happy when the same thing happens to them. I want all this talk to stop right now. I want you to make sure that the other men in the command know that I don't want to hear these innuendos, and I want you to go talk to her and let her know that it's okay. We will survive our deployment. We will find somebody else to do her job, and we will move forward."

It wasn't easy, but I got the words out. Thankfully, I had prayed on it first and asked the Lord to give me the words. Despite my nerves, I just kept reminding myself that if I said nothing,

nothing would change. We would never have a level playing field. I felt that if I didn't speak up, I would do a disservice to my leadership role. I wanted to help pave the way for other women. And the master chief listened. He never again demonized any women in the squadron; at least, not that I heard.

Mind you, I was direct with him, but I wasn't aggressive. I didn't yell or curse, because if I had come across as too aggressive, I would've been called a bitch. On the other hand, if a woman was kind and mild, or worse, whining, they walked all over her. The men didn't have to be so careful about how they said things, but as a woman, I analyzed every word and pitch of my voice before I talked to them. I knew it was important, because I didn't want to make things harder for those who came after me. If the master chief had taken it the wrong way, it could have been bad for all the women.

I was lucky in that I was around people in the Navy who respected my work. And I worked hard so I could continue to rise through the ranks. Even so, one of my father's friends, whose son had been in the Army longer than I had been in the Navy and hadn't reached the same level that I had, questioned my success. He even suggested that I had slept around to get where I was.

It was a ridiculous suggestion because one of the best things about the military is the fairness in advancement. When exams are held, at least in the enlisted ranks, candidates' names don't appear on the exam paper. They are assigned a number, so the examiners don't know whether the exam was taken by a woman or a man. Candidates who pass and score higher than everybody else, advance. If 50 women but only 10 men have high scores, so be it.

My parents didn't know all that, but they knew me well enough to be sure I hadn't earned my position by sleeping around. They cut off the friend who had suggested it and never spoke to him again.

J&C

CHAPTER 4

BALANCING ACT 2:
FAMILY AND CAREER

*"I can do all things through
him who strengthens me."*

—*Philippians 4:13*

H awaii is not only the first place where I lived on my own, but it's also where I met my husband, Nolan. Mutual friends, Don and Lystra, introduced us on Thanksgiving Day.

I met Lystra through Keith, who was also from Trinidad and served in the Marines. He knew I was very selective about my friends and that the few I had were mostly men, but he introduced me to Lystra in the hopes that we'd become friends because she wasn't in the military and was homesick in Hawaii. She was from Trinidad as well and was always calling her mother back home, racking up $600 monthly phone bills, which her husband, Don, was tired of paying. Don didn't like to go out much, but Lystra was an outgoing person. She and I would go shopping or to lunch or we'd party at the club on the base.

One evening Nolan saw me at this club, but he didn't approach me because, as he likes to say, "You had your legs crossed and your nose up in the air with every guy who asked you to dance. I saw you shoo them away, and I didn't want to be one of those. I didn't want to get my feelings hurt!"

Lystra continually tried to find nice guys for me, but none of them were to my taste. So when she said she knew a nice guy who was a friend of Don's, I said, "I've seen the guys you try to select for me, so no thanks. They're not my cup of tea." But she insisted, so I agreed to meet him at the Thanksgiving dinner. Nolan, however, didn't know he was coming to dinner to meet me.

He didn't have a vehicle, so he borrowed his roommate's to drive to Don and Lystra's house. When he left soon after dinner, I assumed that meant he didn't like me. I thought, "Forget him. There are other fish in the sea." What I didn't realize was that since he hadn't known he was coming to meet me, he hadn't planned to stay after dinner. He left early because he had to return his roommate's vehicle and launder his uniform for work the next day.

Nolan, who was in the Air Force, was tall, good-looking, and seemed nice, well mannered, and well spoken. I thought there was potential there, until he left early, that is. At the time, I had only about five friends who knew my phone number, and I'd instructed every one of them not to give it out without my permission. When Don went back to work after the holiday, Nolan asked him, "I really like your friend. You think I can take her out?" Don replied, "Well, I can't give you her number, but I'll call and ask her."

So Don called me up. "You know the guy you met at Thanksgiving? He would like to take you out."

"He can't just take me out. He has to call and ask me himself," I replied.

"Now, how can he do that if he doesn't have your number, which you told me not to give anyone?"

Good point.

"Okay, fine. Go ahead and give him my number."

After that, Nolan called and explained why he'd left early on Thanksgiving. Then, we started talking about everything under the sun, including family and current events. It was refreshing to have a conversation with a man who wasn't all about himself, or sports, or the military. We talked for over an hour. Finally, he asked me out on a date.

I met him for dinner at a Benihana restaurant, and he was the perfect gentleman. He opened the door for me, pulled out my chair, and didn't make any advances. He held my hand while we crossed the street. Again, there was real depth to our conversation. I thought, "Okay, this guy has brains. He has looks. He's respectful. We can work with this."

After that, we started dating. On one of our dates, he told me he'd seen me before, at the club, with Lystra. "I could tell that you're the type of girl you can't just approach and ask out. I knew I had to play my cards right." And he did.

We met in 1981 and got married in 1983, but in between, I left Hawaii. Every three years in the Navy, you get stationed at a new command. The worst thing about Nolan being in the Air Force was that the Navy and the Air Force seldom shared any bases. He had to stay at Hickam Air Force Base in Hawaii while I was sent off to New Jersey.

Before I left Hawaii, my parents came for a visit and I introduced Nolan to them. While they were there, Nolan asked my father for my hand in marriage, and after that, we got engaged.

The day I left, Nolan met me at the airport and gave me a gift. While we were dating, he told me repeatedly that he supported me and would even give me the shirt off his back. When you hear those words, you think it's just something people say, but that wasn't true for Nolan. He framed a Hawaiian shirt that he'd worn on one of our dates and presented it to me. "I told you I would even give you the shirt off my back," he said. And he meant it.

We weren't sure when we'd see each other again after that. Even our wedding date was a big question mark. It was a leap of faith. We were separated for over a year after I left.

My next duty station was in New Jersey. That's where I learned about the Enlisted Commissioning Program, which was a new program. If accepted for it, I could train to become an officer, which had been my original plan when I joined the Navy. I decided to apply and started putting the required materials together for the application. That's when I realized how much I had accomplished, probably because I'd never had a lot of distractions. For example, when I was working on my associate's degree in Hawaii, I was able to go to school full-time during the day and work full-time at night. Until I met Nolan, I didn't have a boyfriend who might interfere with my goals. And I didn't meet Nolan until the last semester before I earned my degree. Even then, I told him, "I really don't have much time for you. I have to finish this up, and then we can start seriously dating." He was willing to wait, and I'm glad he did.

I happened to mention that I was applying for the Enlisted Commissioning Program to a black petty officer who was senior to me, and he tried to discourage me from applying. I don't exactly know why he said, "If I were you, I wouldn't get my hopes up.

You're competing against people who have been in the Navy for far longer." At that juncture, I had fewer than six years in the Navy and I'd made petty officer second class. Every time I'd gone for a higher rank, I'd been successful. My schedule, as far as concerned making a higher rank, was right on the money.

Still, he said, "You're competing with chief petty officers and you're competing with people who have more stuff going on than you. What makes you think you're going to get selected?" I almost bought into what he was saying, but then a light bulb came on and I thought, "You know what? He doesn't approve applications. It's not up to him. What do I have to lose by applying? I'm not going to lose my command. I'm not going to lose my rank. They'll say yes or no. And if they say no, I can find out why I didn't compete well and I can work on those weak points to be ready for my next application." With that in mind, I submitted my application to my division officer and thought that was that.

What I didn't realize was that the officer I had submitted my application to was leaving his position, so while I thought my application was on its way to Washington, it was really still in that officer's in-basket. A new officer recruiter, Lieutenant Commander (LCDR) Penny, checked into the command to replace my old division officer, and he found my application, which his predecessor had left in his in-basket. LCDR Penny came to me to ask what it was, and I told him what I was trying to do. He'd never heard of the Enlisted Commissioning Program, so he looked up the directive for it. When he saw what they expected the application to look like, he brought the instructions to me. "I've spent some time in Washington DC," he said, "and I can tell you if you submit your application the way it is now, it's not even going to get looked at."

"What do you mean?" I asked him.

"Did you get the directive for the program?"

"No, I didn't know about it."

The previous leadership had told me nothing about such a thing. So LCDR Penny handed me the directive. "I want you to take your application and make sure you do everything line by line, based on what they say here," he said. "Put your application in proper order and then give it back to me... By the way, I looked up the date for submission and we have to hurry." I looked at the directive and could tell right away my entire application was out of whack.

So I had to start from scratch. I got the package together and gave it to LCDR Penny, and he looked through it to make sure I had everything done correctly. Then he expedited it up the chain of command for approval. This was hurried stuff, but he stayed on it. He didn't let the application just sit on anybody's desk. He even made sure it was sent by express mail, because I had only one day left at that point to get it to Washington. When he sent it, he asked for a return receipt to be mailed back as confirmation. When that card came back, he brought it to me. "Put this up on your wall for good luck," he said. And I did.

Normally, it took six months or so before applicants received word about their application. I heard back in half that time. I was selected for the program. That receipt stayed on my wall for luck the whole time.

I always say God puts people in your path to help you get where you're supposed to go. It doesn't happen by accident. I also believe that you have to appreciate those people. I can't stand people who say, "Oh, nobody helped me. I'm self-made." No man is self-made. There's always somebody. You may not recognize who they are, but there's always somebody who has helped you achieve something. For me, at that moment, it was LCDR Penny. He could have taken up his new position and told himself that he didn't want to be bothered with my application. Since it hadn't happened on his watch, he didn't care if my application was rejected. Or he could have come to me and said, "Oh, you're too late. The window of opportunity has closed, so apply next year." But he didn't.

I didn't see much of LCDR Penny after that, but I've always remembered him because he made such a huge difference in my life. And that former division officer who had let my application just sit on his desk actually did me a favor. If he had sent in my application the way it was, I never would have been accepted into the program. Because he was negligent, I got the benefit of LCDR Penny's help to submit my application the right way.

So I was going to be an officer. And in the midst of all this, I was planning a wedding all by myself since my husband-to-be was still in Hawaii. I knew I wanted to have the wedding at Huntington Town House in New York, because earlier in life, I'd gone to a wedding there and thought it was the most glamorous place. Nolan said, "You can do anything you want in planning the wedding, but once we pick a date, you have to stick to it. I don't want the date to keep changing or it might never happen."

While I was working in New Jersey, we finally set a date. I originally wanted to be married on my birthday because I'm bad with dates and I figured I'd always remember our anniversary if it was the same day as my birthday. But Nolan said no. He didn't want me to have to share my birthday. So we settled on August 20. I then went to Huntington Town House to make arrangements. Since it was practically a year out, I thought it would be no problem. As it turned out, Huntington Town House was booked for the next five years. They had only one date available in August and it was the twentieth. It was meant to be.

Around that time, Nolan decided to leave the Air Force because we couldn't be stationed together since I was entering the officer program and didn't know where I'd end up. Back then, the military would tell you that since your spouse "didn't come in your duffel bag"—in other words, he or she wasn't issued to you by the military—your separations were just something you had to deal with. You couldn't do much about it. There used to be a saying among the Navy wives that home is where the Navy sends you. Nolan and I wanted to make our home together, so he left the Air Force to be able to join me wherever I ended up.

He didn't get a chance to come out east until it was almost time for us to get married. He came about a week before, and that's when he saw all the planning I'd done. The only selection he made was his best man, who was his older brother. He didn't even know the other groomsmen. His mother had left his father when he was young and his father had died not long after. He and his brother were raised by their grandmother, and aunt and uncle, but when he went into the service, he didn't have much communication with them. So his mother and brother were the only people he invited to the wedding.

We got married on August 20, and everything went off without a hitch. The only complication was that I invited both my adoptive mother, Jean, and my birth mother, Yvonne. Ninety-nine percent of the wedding guests knew me as Jean's child, and she was nervous that my biological mother might somehow inject herself into the forefront of the event. So, without telling Jean, I went to Yvonne and asked her if she would play a background role during my wedding to let Jean be the mother of the bride. Yvonne understood, which I appreciated. If she was hurt by it, she never let on. She was very gracious and sympathetic to Jean's feelings.

Huntington Town House offered a private room for the bride and groom, which had a close-circuit TV on which they could watch guests entertaining themselves in the grand ballroom. We had our own bathroom there and I had a maître d' assigned to me. My husband and I were ready to party in this room by ourselves, but Jean wouldn't leave my side. It was a really special and emotional day for her. Thankfully, my husband was great with my parents. He treated them as if they were his own family. He never once suggested my mother should leave or anything like that. We would just look at each other and smile, as if to say, "Well, this is her day too."

Nolan and I spent Sunday, the day after our wedding, with my parents. On Monday we started driving to New Mexico because I had to report to my command there on Tuesday. We drove nonstop cross-country to Albuquerque. That was our honeymoon. We were supposed to go to the Poconos, and, in fact, Nolan had already put a deposit on a room there. But when I

I married my best friend and strongest supporter.

was selected for the officer program, I was given an exact date on which I had to report to school. There was just no time for the Poconos. So we didn't have a honeymoon for 10 years. We did, eventually, go to the Poconos, though. I surprised Nolan with a trip there on our tenth anniversary.

I'd received my associate's degree in Hawaii, but I had to finish my bachelor's degree in New Mexico before I could get my commission as an officer. I attended the University of New Mexico in Albuquerque and majored in political science. At first I thought I'd major in chemistry because I wanted to become a doctor. My parents loved the idea of their daughter becoming a doctor and it's what I thought I wanted too until I realized how much studying it entailed. Nolan was able to join the Air National Guard in New Mexico and continue his time in service, so he worked during the day. I attended school during the day, after which I went to work and then on to study hall, and the lab, during the evening. I was away all the time. One day Nolan told me, "All I see is the back of your head. I wake up in the morning to the back of your head. I go to sleep at night and there's the back of your head."

Because I wanted to enjoy my new marriage, and because I wasn't sure what I would do with a chemistry degree in the Navy, I started looking at other degree majors that wouldn't be as time consuming. One of my fellow ROTC members, who was a political science student, had also switched his major. He described his courses. I thought they sounded pretty interesting, so I went to the administration and asked if I could transfer with the credits I already had. They said, "Sure, you have plenty of credits to do that. You'll be finished in no time." That sounded great to me. And that's how I ended up with a political science degree.

After that, I transferred to Newport, Rhode Island, for the U.S. Navy Officer Candidate School, where I went through a tough, 16-week training course. I was in a mixed environment where half the class was new officer recruits and the rest were prior military folks like me who had gone through the system and were now transferring from enlisted to officer rank. All the units were run by a commander, who was just someone assigned to the role, not someone with any sort of leadership training.

Our unit's commander was new to the military. He was a gung-ho type, really rough and rude. He would say such things as, "If you flunk out of Officer Candidate School, you're going to go pump gas for Mom and Dad." But he didn't know what he was talking about. If I had flunked out, I'd still have had a job in the military; I would just have reverted to my enlisted rank. He would also do such things as leave a Coke can in the hallway to see who didn't pick it up. Then he'd fuss and yell at that person. It was like boot camp all over again but with a different twist because he claimed he was showing us what the "real military" was all about, whereas I already knew what actual military life was like. It was comical but also frustrating because I couldn't say anything. I would have been canned in a heartbeat. I just had to play the game.

It was knife-and-fork school, so to speak. A lot of our training wasn't related to the military system that I knew. I guess they figured the training had to be different from that of the enlisted boot camp to make sure we weren't too much like the subordinates who'd be working for us. I didn't embrace that idea because I came from the subordinate rank. In my experience, mustangs— which is what the military calls officers who start out as enlisted service members—are highly regarded by those who work for them because mustangs have been in the trenches and can relate.

Despite those things, I made it through officer school pretty smoothly. After that, I hoped to be stationed back in New Mexico because I was an aviation maintenance officer, designation 1520, and there was a 1520 billet at Kirkland Air Force Base, near where I'd gone to college. We'd purchased a house about six months prior to my graduation with that very idea in mind. That home in Rio Rancho, New Mexico, was our first. I spoke with my placement officer and put feelers out about getting a spot at Kirkland, but they had closed the position there by the time I graduated officer candidate school. So I ended up in Jacksonville, Florida.

I didn't even know where Jacksonville was when I was assigned there. I didn't want to go, but I didn't have a choice. Nolan stayed in New Mexico, so again, we were separated. After about six months, as our squadron was returning from a detachment to Puerto Rico, the commanding officer, who knew I hadn't seen my husband in some time, said to me, "We have a flight going out to California. I see no reason why we can't stop in New Mexico and drop you off on the way. Then we can pick you up on our way back." You could do things like that in those days. I was so touched that he was looking out for me.

We landed in New Mexico in a P-3 aircraft, which is a four-engine prop plane. I was just an ensign at the time, which was an O-1 rank—higher than an enlisted, but the lowest officer rank. But when the plane dropped me off, the people on the deck thought some big-time officer must be coming in, so they rolled out the red carpet and met me on the stairs.

It was during that visit home that I became pregnant with our firstborn. It was hard to be separated from my husband so often, but to get through it we just had to trust each other. One thing about my husband is that that he has always been secure in who he is and committed to supporting me. And he doesn't use words only to show me this. He shows me with both words and deeds.

That's why, when I found out I was pregnant, he decided to come to Jacksonville. I told him to not worry about coming because I thought I would have a short-term tour there and then be able to negotiate a transfer to somewhere else. I figured I would have the baby and join him, hopefully, in New Mexico if I could arrange it. But he said, "Jen, I'm not going to let you have this baby by yourself."

"What's wrong with that? I don't need you to have this baby," I protested.

But he put his foot down. "I'm going to speak to my command and ask if I can get a transfer to the Air National Guard in Jacksonville. If not, we will just make do. Either way, I'm coming over there." I was living in the barracks at the time, but when I got pregnant, I was able to apply for base housing. He joined me when I was about six months pregnant.

We ended up staying in Jacksonville for the birth of all three of our children. When I had my first two, Nolan II, after his father, and then Nyckie, two years later, I was on shore command, which was easier because I was stationary and didn't have to travel. But when my son was two and my daughter was not even a year old, I was assigned a new command in a deploying squadron, which meant traveling away from home on six-month deployments.

I'd been on deployments before, but it was nothing like going on deployments when I had young children. But again, I didn't have a choice. There were lots of people in my situation and we all just had to toughen up. In the military at that time, having young children wasn't enough of a reason to be transferred to another command or to not go on deployments. Women were not forced to go on deployments if they were pregnant, but once the child was born, they had to officially designate someone who would care for the child when they were away. If both parents were in the military, they had to designate a third person in case they were both away at the same time.

My husband was on full-time guard duty with the National Guard, but thankfully, his job was stationary most of the time, and we were usually able to coordinate our schedules. The only time we had an issue was after 9/11, when he had to stop what he was doing and was sent away immediately. I was in Tallahassee, working as the executive director of the Florida Department of Veteran's Affairs. He called me. "We're shipping out," he said, "and I don't know where or when I'm coming back." At times like that we just had to ask for help.

My husband was always very good with the kids. When they were small, he'd get up in the middle of the night and take care of them, even change diapers. I would wake up rested, believing the kids hadn't woken up during the night. "Yes, they did," he would say. As good as he was with them, my first deployment was very hard on him. He had to look after two very young children all on his own. He didn't even know how to comb our daughter's hair. He's not an outgoing person, so it was a difficult for him to seek care for them when he needed to.

Before I went on deployment, I tried to put the kids in daycare on the base, but there was something there my son didn't like. You can imagine the tug on a mother when she's trying to drop her kid off at daycare and he's screaming and hollering and holding on to the car so he won't have to go in. He kept saying, "Don't take me and my sister in there!" But I had to go to work, so what was I going to do? These are the trials of any parent. I called a friend who lived on the base, and she was able to keep them for the day. Fortunately, her sister ran a daycare out of her home, and she took the kids after that. To this day, I don't know why little Nolan reacted the way he did, because he was too young to explain it to me, but he just didn't want to go in that daycare center and I wasn't about to make him.

It was a lot to juggle, especially when the kids got sick. Then, when they got older, we had things like school plays, soccer games, dance recitals, gymnastics, and football to work into the schedule. We were the type of family who did things together, similar to how my parents had raised me. Unlike how I grew up, however, my kids did have friends. We allowed that, but we didn't allow them to sleep over at anybody's house. We provided them with a very controlled environment and kept them busy. All my kids started preschool when they were two and participated in lots of activities outside school when they were older. When they had summer vacations or were out of school, they always had stuff to do. I always went to the Scholastic store and bought additional work for them to do while they were home. We went to church and worked in the yard together. They all had chores to do. People who knew us would say my kids had more fun going to school than they did on vacation because we kept them so busy. It was very much like the way I had been raised, except that I was raised as an only child, and my kids, at least, had each other.

I was dealing with so much, as a matter of fact, that when my 10-year mark in the Navy came around, I seriously thought about retiring. I worried about how often my job took me away from my family, and besides that, I had become very tired of the "boy's club." Despite my achievements, there were always those who tried to undermine the women officers. Many of the chief petty officers acted as if we didn't know as much as they did, which meant we had to work even harder to be appreciated. If we even sneezed, there were those who accused us of slacking off because we were women. I was always biting my tongue, because I'd seen women branded as troublemakers who couldn't get along with the establishment, just because they complained about the sexism. The negativism continued nonstop, and with everything else happening at home, I felt pressured.

My friend Cynt, who was a Lt. Commander, convinced me to take a step back and look at the situation. She said she knew it was difficult, but I should look at how far I'd come. She pointed out that I was doing as well or better than others, so why would I give anyone the opportunity to break me?

I decided to give my life in the Navy one more chance, and I'm glad I did. Circumstances didn't necessarily get easier, but I think I got better at juggling everything. I spent another 10 years in the Navy after that, which led me to what would be my next career—in politics.

gsl

CHAPTER 5

BALANCING ACT 3: AGING PARENTS

*"Honor your father and mother; which is
the first commandment with a promise."*

—*Ephesians 6:2*

When I started going on deployments again, my mother decided to retire so she could help out with the children. Initially, she came down just when we needed her, but then she and my father decided to move to Florida. They built a house across the street from us, and after that, it was a whole lot easier on my husband when I had to go away.

In 1991 I became pregnant again. Early in my pregnancy I was scheduled to go on deployment, but I didn't mention my pregnancy for fear of being stigmatized, as I'd seen happen to so many women. On deployment, I did heavy lifting and things that may have led to my miscarriage. The pains started after I came back. I went to the doctor and he told me I had lost the baby, but he wanted me to pass the fetus naturally, without a D&C. I was taking my dad to the eye doctor when the awful labor pains started. When we got to the eye doctor's office, I went into the bathroom and passed the fetus. It was terrible. I vowed that I would never again sacrifice my health or my family for my job.

The loss took a toll on my dad. He had been looking forward to that pregnancy because, in addition to never having had children of their own, my parents were in New York when my first two were born. But Jean had been through her own miscarriage and I think mine brought back sad memories. My father was so upset that when I became pregnant again, with Necho, he was nervous the whole time. He never wanted to talk about the pregnancy until Necho was about to come out.

It was nice to have grandparents so close when the kids were young, but unfortunately, it wasn't long before I noticed my mother's declining health. It started with diabetes, heart problems, and hypertension. That they moved so close ended up being a blessing in ways I hadn't foreseen. If my mother had stayed in New York, I firmly believe she would have died sooner than she did. She never saw the need to take care of herself. But because I could see what was happening, I was able to go with her to the doctor and make sure she was taking care of her herself properly.

That became another balancing act because here I was, taking care of my young family while also taking care of my aging parents. My father was from the old school, which meant he didn't cook for himself, he didn't grocery shop, he didn't wash his clothes, or iron, or do any "womanly stuff." My mother had him spoiled. He too had retired when they moved down, and it was a difficult change for both of them because they were so used to working all the time. My mother always felt he was bothering her and she wanted to get him out of the house, so I found him a maintenance job at the Navy exchange on base. There, he was able to fix things, man the warehouse, and arrange store displays. That kind of work he loved, but when it came to housework, he was not about to pitch in.

Then, I started noticing more strange behavior from my mother. Initially, I thought she had simple memory loss due to normal aging. It was a while before I realized she had Alzheimer's. I had my first big scare when she was supposed to pick me up from the beauty salon near the base. I gave her clear directions on how to get there. They were very easy: a straight line and then a left and a right. She was supposed to pick me up at 4:00 p.m., but 4:00 p.m. came and went and she wasn't there. We didn't have cell phones as we do today, so she stopped at a payphone and called me at about 5:00 p.m. She was lost.

I asked if she had passed the base, and she said no, so I gave her directions from where I thought she was. The problem was, she had already passed the base and just didn't remember. Five o'clock turned into seven o'clock and she still hadn't shown up. Around that time, there had been a number of carjackings in the area, so I was really starting to worry. I called home and asked my dad if she had made it back and he said no, so I called my husband and asked him to come and pick me up. We went home, and still no mom.

I called the police station after that to find out if anybody had reported a car on the side of the road, or an accident, but there was no news. At 10:00 p.m. I called the Clay County Sheriff and was told I had to go to Jacksonville to file a missing persons report since that's where the salon was located and where she was likely to have gone missing. So that night, I drove to Jacksonville where I met Officer Vasser, who decided to put out a silver alert on my mother.

His decision to put out a silver alert, which goes out nation-wide, made all the difference. At about two in the morning we got a call that she'd been spotted. At that point I was sure the police would tell me they'd found her dead somewhere, but she was in Sanford, which is two-and-a-half hours south of where we lived. "What is she doing there?" I asked. The officer told me they were concerned because she didn't know her name or where she was.

My husband and I drove to Sanford immediately after the call and met her at the hospital. The doctor told us then that her cognitive system was not functioning properly and recommended that we take her to her primary physician to have more tests done. I did so, but the tests were fine. I still kept an eye on her, though, and I saw more deterioration as time went by. She would leave the stove on, for example. On one occasion, she even left a small fire burning in her kitchen and came across the street to see me. I was in my kitchen, preparing dinner, when she walked in with soot in her hair. I asked what it was, and she told me she didn't know. It looked like charred paper, so I ran across the street. The fire was still burning on the stove and I had to put it out.

After that, she started having trouble driving. She would put the car in forward instead of reverse to back out of the garage and ended up running into the freezer. So I hid her car keys, but she started wandering off. She would say something such as, "I'm going to see my mother," pick up her pocketbook, and walk out of the house. I had to arrange home care for her because my husband and I were still in the military, working all day, and my dad wasn't about to stay at home to watch her. A couple of times when she walked away, he came over to tell me, but he wouldn't go to look for her himself. He didn't think that was his job.

Pretty soon she wasn't able to bathe herself, so I had to assist her. I had to prepare their meals because she couldn't remember simple things such as what a tomato was. I made all their meals and put them in plastic containers in the freezer, particularly if I was going to be gone for a while, but I would come back and see all the meals still there. I told my dad all he had to do was warm up the food in the microwave, but he wouldn't even do that. Again, not his job.

I once had a detachment that took me from home for a few weeks. When I came back, I found that my mother had a urinary tract infection because my father hadn't made sure she was properly washed. That was when she really deteriorated. She started losing her ability to walk, and it was a downward slope from there.

In the midst of all this, I finally retired from the military so I could campaign for a Congressional seat. It was a challenge seat, and the incumbent was very unresponsive to her constituency, which, at that time, was one of the poorest.

I'd been working as an admiral's aide when I was first thrust into the political realm. Admiral Kevin Delaney had me doing a lot of liaison work with elected members, and that's when I learned about this particular representative for the district where the base was located. As I traveled the district more and more for my job, I saw all these pockets of poverty that the incumbent representative and others were turning a blind eye to, particularly in the minority areas. The surrounding districts were booming economically. They had a good quality of life and good schools. I wondered why the incumbent hadn't done something about the poverty in her district if she had had the same opportunities as the other members of Congress had for their districts. I made the decision that when I retired, I would run for that Congressional seat so I could try to make a positive difference for the constituents there. When my 20 years of service came around, which is when military personnel can choose to retire, I did just that. The time seemed right to make a change.

That's how I ended up running my first political campaign while also raising young children and caring for my aging parents. It was a lot to juggle, and what suffered was me. Time for me went out the window. I didn't sleep much, typically, only two or three hours each morning. I can't even say "each night," because I was going to sleep in the morning and waking up in the morning. I was also traveling a lot. There were about 170 miles between district points, from Jacksonville all the way to Orlando, and the area encompassed a lot of smaller communities with only two-lane roads. But I had to get out and meet the constituents if I was going to make a dent. The incumbent had the advantage, of course, because everyone knew who she was.

It was a tough time, but I got to meet great people along the way. Many of them didn't know me, but because of my credentials, believed in me and stepped up to the plate for me. For example, there was an individual named Duane Ottenstroer, who was introduced to me by a mutual friend. Duane was a wealthy businessman who knew nothing of me at first, but he took the time to meet with me and did his homework on my background. Because of him, I was able to get funding for my campaign. He was a power broker who brought other power brokers to the table to make donations. Without him, I wouldn't have had the resources to run the race.

Unfortunately, the resources I did have were somewhat stifled by the Republican establishment. In fact, some establishment Republicans financially supported my opponent. The vice chair of the state Republican Party didn't want me to run against the incumbent Democrat because he didn't want me to bring to the polls a lot of black voters who might vote for me but might not vote for George Bush, who was running for his first term as president. In fact, the Republican establishment preferred that black voters stay home and not vote at all.

I didn't win, but I did get 42 percent of the vote. I also had more individual contributors than my opponent had as an incumbent. I can only guess what might have happened if the Republican National Committee (RNC) had gotten behind my campaign, but the RNC kept moving the carrot. They would say, "We have the presidential campaign going on so most of our money has to go to that, but next quarter, let's see how much money you raise." Every quarter they asked me to raise more and I would raise more—and from individuals, not political action committees or big corporations. But no matter how much more I raised, the RNC would always say, "Well, let's see what happens next quarter."

Ironically, although they tried to discourage me from running because of the concern that I'd bring out black voters, my campaign ended up being a positive for George W. Bush. After the 2000 election, a lot of the issues with the hanging and dimpled chads occurred in my Florida district. When the counts and recounts were completed, George Bush won by only 537 votes. That's all the election boiled down to.

In one part of my district, 27,000 ballots were discarded because two presidential candidates had been selected. When people were bused to the polls, they were instructed to vote for Gore and Brown—Corrine Brown, my opponent. The problem was that a certain Harry Browne was running as the Libertarian candidate for the presidency. As a result, a lot of people accidentally voted for Gore and the wrong Browne. And their ballots were discounted because of it. It's been estimated that Gore would have captured 90 percent of those 27,000 ballots that were rejected. Had I not been on the ticket as a black Republican opponent, they wouldn't have had to tell people to vote for Brown, which means voters probably wouldn't have made that mistake. And Gore would have won the election by a good margin.

Despite the loss, it was a positive experience because it really opened my eyes to the needs of the community. After my campaign, I got involved with a number of boards to assist troubled children and families, and I dedicated a lot of time to mentoring students in the Junior Achievement and the YMCA Black Achiever's programs. When I did my mentoring, I would take my kids along because I wanted them to see that there were young people out there who didn't have what they had. It was my hope that when they were older, my kids would want to give back to their community as well. I'm starting to see that, now they've all become young adults. My oldest son, Nolan, for example, plays professional football and donates his time and money to various causes, particularly children's causes. He and I participate together in the NFL Play 60, which teaches kids about physical fitness and proper nutrition. Running for office really showed me that I could contribute in other ways, outside the military, and still make a difference.

Those months when I was running my political campaign were a roller-coaster ride, and my mother's declining health was a big part of it. I arranged for a couple of ladies to take care of her after she started losing her ability to walk. Despite the help, she suffered another infection and entirely lost her ability to walk and communicate. This is where my regret comes in. I was handling so much and making so many decisions quickly that I didn't involve my dad as much as I probably should have. I took my mom to the hospital to be treated for the infection, after which the doctors told me she would have to go into a nursing home unless I had someone at home to care for her full-time. I knew my dad wasn't going to do it, so I had her transferred to a nearby nursing home without talking to him.

Afterward, I went to the base where my dad was working to let him know. I immediately saw the disappointment on his face. He never said anything, but I think it hit him like a ton of bricks. I think he still assumed that my mom would come out of the hospital and everything would be fine. She had always been a very strong woman. She took care of her own affairs and she took care of him. It was hard for him to picture her needing his help. Had I included my dad in the decision, I think I could have made the transition a bit smoother for him. Mom was in the nursing home for only about six months before she suffered another stroke and died of heart failure.

Almost immediately afterward, my father's health started to deteriorate. As it had with my mom, it didn't really hit me until something major happened. Dad didn't like going to the doctor, but he kept telling me he was having a hard time urinating, so I told him he needed to get it checked out. His answer was that every time people go to a doctor, they come out worse than they were before. I didn't want to push because he'd just lost my mom, but when he told me he was urinating clumps of blood, I said he didn't have a choice. I made a doctor's appointment and that's when he was diagnosed with prostate cancer.

I didn't notice his hallucinations until he called me one night. By this time we had moved from the house across the street from my dad's house to a place about a mile away. When I picked up the phone, he said, "Jen, did you invite people over from the church?" I said, "No. I wouldn't invite anyone to your house without telling you." He said, "They are here and have been for a while and I can't get them to leave."

My husband and I were very concerned, so we dashed over to his house. My dad lived in a cul-de-sac. We didn't see any cars leaving as we approached, but when we arrived at the house, he told us his visitors had just left. I said, "Nobody left, Dad."

"You didn't see them out there?" he asked.

"No, the street is dark. There's not even a car on the road."

"There's one!" he said pointing. "See that one over there? It doesn't have feet and it just has a head for a table. And see the ones outside? They're digging up the yard!" My husband and I looked at each other knowing there was something very wrong with this picture.

I couldn't believe my dad was now losing his faculties too. During this period, Aunt Daisy was coming down fairly regularly with her husband to pay small visits. They would stay a few days and then go back to New York. We were about to go on a family vacation when the incident with my dad occurred. I didn't want to leave him by himself, so I called Aunt Daisy to ask if she would stay with him. But she said, "Carl is fine. There's nothing wrong with him."

I thought that was a little strange, but I still didn't want to leave my dad alone, so I called Mr. Louie, a friend of his from the islands, and asked if he would look in on my dad while we were gone. He said he would. But then, when we got back, we found my Aunt Daisy visiting Dad even though she'd said it wasn't necessary. What I didn't know was that she and her husband had taken the opportunity to have themselves named as beneficiaries of my father's life insurance policy, among other things. He'd had me named as his beneficiary on everything, but they'd persuaded him to take my name off his bank accounts, his CDs, and so on, and put their names on instead. They'd even hired an attorney to help them behind my back. As it turned out, that attorney was disbarred some years later.

One morning soon after that, Aunt Daisy called me to ask if my father was at my house. I told her no, and she said he was nowhere to be found. So I started driving around the neighborhood to look for him and eventually spotted him walking along the highway in his pajamas and bedroom slippers. He thought someone was chasing him and that people were at his house waiting to take him away. He didn't want to come with me, so I had to talk to him for a while to reassure him that everything was okay. When I finally got him back to the house, Aunt Daisy just laughed it off. I knew I had to get him back to the doctor and I told Aunt Daisy I would make an appointment. But the next day,

Aunt Daisy and her husband took Dad on a Greyhound bus back to their house in New York before I could get him to the doctor.

I found out when I knocked on Dad's door the next morning and no one answered. Aunt Daisy also had my father change the locks on the house so I couldn't get in with my keys. I called a girl who had befriended my dad at work and asked if she knew where he was. She said, "Didn't Daisy tell you? She took him to New York."

It was hours later that Aunt Daisy called to let me know they'd arrived in New York. I asked how she could take my dad on such a long trip in his condition. She didn't have an explanation. I told her I'd never felt so betrayed in my entire life. She didn't have an answer for that either. That was the last time we spoke until I got a call from my dad's other sister, my Aunt Moislie, telling me he had fallen down the steps at Aunt Daisy's house. He was in the ICU at the hospital, unconscious, with a blood clot in his head.

I firmly believe that my dad fell because he was in an unfamiliar environment. His own house had only one story, so he wasn't used to stairs. He was obviously having hallucinations of some sort, which I think were caused by cancer spreading to his brain. But I'll never know because I didn't get a chance to take him to the doctor and Aunt Daisy obviously hadn't taken him before it was too late.

I immediately went to New York to see my dad. A good friend of my mother's took me to the hospital. It just so happened that while I was in the ICU, Aunt Daisy came in. She was stunned to see me and asked what I was doing there. She didn't know my other aunt had called to tell me what had happened. I didn't blow up as I wanted to. I just told her that I was there to see my father.

I discovered then that my aunt had not told the medical staff that my father had prostate cancer or that he'd had hallucinations. They had him strapped to his bed because, even though he was unconscious, he would move around a lot and they were afraid he'd fall out. He was probably having more hallucinations. He never did wake up after that. He died of a heart attack while still in the ICU.

By the time he passed, I was back in Florida. Aunt Daisy didn't even bother to let me know about the funeral. My aunt in Trinidad called to tell me. My parents had discussed with me how they wanted to be buried. They both wanted to be cremated, and I still have my mom's ashes in an urn at my home. My father wanted the same thing, but Aunt Daisy didn't believe in cremation, so my dad's wishes weren't honored. He's buried way out in Long Island, New York, far away from where my aunt lives, in Brooklyn, and no one goes to see his grave. Because Aunt Daisy was not a member of a church, she had to hire a priest that she didn't know to give his eulogy.

Even though Aunt Daisy made it pretty clear she didn't want me there, I went to the funeral and spoke about my parents, about how they had loved and taken care of me, and about how much I appreciated everything they had done for me. It was very hard to see my dad go out that way. He didn't have his wishes upheld. He didn't have his own priest. Then, to be buried in an area where no one went to see his grave . . .

After my father's burial, Aunt Daisy and her husband filed a claim in court to acquire my parents' home. That's when I really started to understand what had happened and why. We had to go to a hearing before a judge to settle the claim. I had only recently discovered that Aunt Daisy had persuaded my father to change his will and accounts, but the deed to my parents' house was still set up so the house would pass to me.

The first question out of the judge's mouth was, "Are you related to Mrs. Carroll?" Aunt Daisy said she was not. I was floored. I told the judge that she was my aunt, my dad's sister. She told the judge she wasn't.

That's when the reality hit me that this woman had never accepted me as part of the family. Because I was adopted, I wasn't really family in her eyes. Daisy had three daughters of her own and I think she felt that if my father had wanted a girl to raise, he should have adopted one from his own family.

The judge also asked her if my dad had other siblings, to which she answered yes. He then asked why she was the only one of these siblings who felt she should get all of what my father had. She couldn't answer that question.

The judge finally said he didn't know why we were there because the house clearly belonged to me. Daisy was stunned. Except for their property, contents, and my mother's jewelry, she took everything. I didn't think it was worth the trouble to challenge her on the will or any of the rest of it.

That remained the worst betrayal I had ever experienced in my life until what happened in my political life to come. It really sunk my heart. This woman lived in our house with her family when she first moved to the United States. She and her family were always around and my mother was very kind to her. All that time, she thought of me as an outsider, and I didn't even know it. Thankfully, the other members of my dad's family aren't like her and we're all still close.

CHAPTER 6

LIVING A
POLITICAL LIFE

*"But those who hope in the Lord will renew
their strength. They will soar on wings
like eagles; they will run and not grow
weary; they will walk and not be faint."*

—*Isaiah 40:31*

I was serving as the executive director of the Florida Department of Veteran Affairs when a member of the Florida House of Representatives asked me if I would consider running for his seat because he was leaving to run for tax collector in Duval County. He'd seen me run my Congressional campaign and knew my background and credentials, so he sought me out. It was a bit difficult to say yes at first because I knew how much work my previous campaign had been and how hard it was to lose. I wasn't sure I wanted to put my family through all that again.

My husband is not a political person. He doesn't care anything about politics. His focus is on family, work, and church. He was very hurt by how my congressional race ended because he knew my passion and what I wanted to do for people. In his mind, he couldn't understand why everyone hadn't seen the goodness in his wife. He was really turned off by politics as a result.

When this opportunity came up, I felt I had to ask my family first. Despite some reservations, they decided to support me if that was what I wanted. And they helped with the campaign, even the kids, who were still young. They put on rollerblades and went door to door to hand out literature. They stuffed, stamped, and licked envelopes. They attended functions with me and would wave signs at events.

Fortunately, things ended differently this time. I was more in control of my race and I stayed as far away as I could from the lobbyists and political consultants in Tallahassee, which initially made them think my campaign wasn't going to be successful. But I had a great, energetic team of young people on board, including Matt Justice, Brian Graham, Bill and Mary Ellen Ludeking, Roger Mcgaha, Rick Bebout, and Marie McGee. These were my volunteers until I was able to raise some resources from local folks and people who believed in me. Mr. Ottenstroer, who had been so helpful in my Congressional campaign, again stepped up to help.

Sadly, in politics, sooner or later, you have to deal with the "whisper" campaign. You never know where the whispers are coming from, but people put information out there—true or not—that's meant to sabotage you. The whisper campaign in Tallahassee was that my campaign wasn't going anywhere. I wasn't going to win because I was a black woman in an area of rednecks. The whisper was those white rednecks would surely vote for my opponent, who was a white woman and had already run a successful campaign to become a school board member.

Those whispers almost caused our resources to dry up. But one thing the whisper mongers underestimated was that people remembered how I had run my congressional race. It wasn't about the color of my skin; it was about my qualifications and the person they saw on the campaign trail.

It so happened that, one day, while I was walking the district, knocking on doors, a lobbyist and former state senator showed up. He lived in the district and didn't like my opponent, so he had a personal axe to grind. Then another lobbyist arrived because he had heard the whispers in Tallahassee and he was curious. As we were walking the district, both these men could see how people were gladly opening their doors to me, and they were stunned. What was happening didn't match the rumors that were spreading in Tallahassee. Afterward, they went back to Tallahassee and spread the word that "People know her, she has her act together, her campaign is fine, and she's going to win."

There were still naysayers, but we kept the energy high until the night of the election. Now, one of my faults is that I don't let myself enjoy the moment when I'm successful. I work hard to achieve things, and when I do, it's as if I say to myself, "Okay, this is done. Let's move on to the next thing."

There I was on the night of the election, my family was with me, and the results were coming in. I wouldn't let myself go, because I remembered the disappointment after my congressional races. I was ahead early on, but the same thing had happened before. I'd been ahead, and then, all of a sudden, my lead started slipping.

But this time the numbers kept looking good and people were saying there was no way my opponent could catch up. Then it was over, the race was called, and I still wouldn't let myself enjoy the moment. It just didn't feel real, until I had the call from Governor Jeb Bush congratulating me on the win. It was surreal, like an out-of-body experience, because everybody around me was joyous and celebrating, but I still didn't feel celebratory. Finally, I just had to snap out of it. Then, all these people who *hadn't* supported me started coming to my headquarters to congratulate me. It's a good thing I'm not someone who harbors malice. So many people told me they'd supported me, anyone would think I had won 100 percent of the votes.

I was the first black Republican woman ever elected to the Florida legislature. Two counties made up my district. As it turned out, in the county where they said the white rednecks would never vote for me, I received over 85 percent of the votes. In the larger county, I received over 61 percent of the votes. It just goes to show you that you can't listen to whispers or to the so-called experts. You have to believe in yourself. Although hard times come and you don't always get what you want when you want it, I firmly believe the Lord knows what's best for us. We just have to be obedient, pray, and keep trying. Throughout all my adversities, what have brought me out of the storm have been my faith, prayer, and my strong family support.

After that, I spent a little over seven years in the Florida legislature. Elections are held every two years, and I was unopposed in every election after the first.

I always appreciated the opportunity the voters gave me to serve, but it was certainly another balancing act. Much like the military, there was a good old boys' network to contend with. After Connie Mack left to run for Congress, the then speaker of the house, Johnnie Byrd, put me in Mack's former position as deputy majority leader. Even in a leadership position, however, I never felt as if I were truly "in" leadership. I still felt that closed door. I was never allowed in the back room with the fellas when they were making deals. Only a handful of people had that kind of power, and I never got to be one of them.

I was not one of those who buddied up with leadership, lobbyists, or money people. I didn't go golfing or socializing unless we were doing a fundraising event. I never used my position and connections to gain wealth or power. I did my work, and when I had finished, I went home to my family. In that sense, I wasn't a typical politician, and I didn't truly fit in the world of politics. I think those who are entering politics need to know that if they really want to be seated at the table, they're going to have to play the game. I didn't like the game much, because it just wasn't me. I didn't get into politics to make myself rich or powerful, or to have a title and position that made me feel I was somebody. I entered politics to do my part to make things better for others. I made a commitment to myself and to the Lord to stay humble and always remember why I was in that position in the first place, which was because of the people who put me there.

There was an instance early on that made it pretty clear that I would do things my own way. Some lobbyists and supporters who have contributed to a successful political campaign assume that the winning candidate will do everything they want that politician to do. Well, I wasn't like that. Whenever someone asked me to support a measure, I would want to hear both sides of the argument. One particular bill came through committee that was being lobbied by a former representative and financial supporter of mine. The bill would have been good for his client in Miami, but when I listened as it was presented, something just didn't sound right. So I called my district city manager and county commissioner to ask how it would impact my district. They called back to let me know that it would impact my county in a negative way.

This supporter assumed he had my vote, even though he had never asked for it. He thought the bill was going to pass, so he left before the vote. Well, I voted against the bill and it failed in committee. He was furious with me. He called and asked, "How could you vote against me without telling me?"

"First, you never asked how I was going to vote," I said. "And second, how dare you assume that just because you gave me a campaign contribution, I'm going to be some kind of lapdog and do whatever you want."

I was angry, but the longer I served in the legislature, the more I realized that this sort of arrangement happens all the time. In fact, when some politicians are against a bill that one of their allies is behind, rather than stand up and vote against it, all too often, they just walk out of committee and do not vote at all. It's not a good field to be in if you want to stay true to what you believe.

Another situation arose with my education bill that was designed to help reading teachers avoid spending time and money on obtaining duplicate credentials. The existing requirement for reading teacher certification meant many teachers had to go back to school, even if they already had a master's degree. The additional course they were required to take took money out of their pockets and time away from their families. The new bill called for removing that requirement for teachers who had already taken the necessary coursework while earning their master's degree.

I was prepared to present my bill on the floor, but every time it came up, it was pulled. I finally went to the education committee chairperson and asked why this was happening. He explained that one of our members, who was in leadership, had a bill she wanted to present to the committee, so she was holding my bill hostage to get her own bill heard in the senate committee.

I think that if I'd truly understood what politics was all about, I would have pursued something else, because that's not me. I don't like the undermining. I don't like the dishonesty or the backstabbing. I'm not interested in manipulating folks. My bill did receive a hearing in the end because I went to the senate committee chairperson and he honored my wish to have it heard. But that could never have been the end of the wheeling and dealing. Once people give a candidate support, most expect something back. It was a lesson learned. I was going to have to be very careful if I didn't want to end up in a compromised position.

At the end of a session, for example, leadership would always ask, "What are your priority bills?" In the first year, I gave them my list, but that didn't mean leadership would help me push those bills through. It was just information they could use, like little pawns in a chess game, so they could wheel and deal. So, the next year when they asked me, I said I had no priority bills. I wasn't going to give away my cards like that. It just never seemed to matter to those people that the bills might contain something of importance to citizens. So I figured I'd work my tail off to get done what I thought was important, and if my bills didn't pass, that was the fault of the game players.

That teachers' bill eventually passed but was vetoed by Governor Crist. It was politics all over again. A group didn't want the measure and convinced the governor to shoot it down.

I took the job the citizens gave me very seriously, but I think one of the things that constituents don't realize is that a representative's job is part-time. The money paid to members of the legislature isn't enough to sustain their families, so they have to have additional employment. Besides serving in the legislature, I opened hair salon franchises in two locations in my district, employing up to 25 people, and started a consulting business. So that became a balancing act too. If a constituent has a need or an event they want their representative to attend, it's very hard for their representative to say, "Well, I just work from this month to this month. I'll see you when I come back." Their needs are present all year round, and representatives have to figure out how to balance them with their need to make enough money to support their families.

In my legislative office I had two staffers with whom I was very engaged on a daily basis. They helped me keep in contact with my constituents by responding to their requests, arranging speeches and town hall meetings, doing surveys before the legislative session, informing the public about what I was doing, clearing up any misinformation about bills, and so forth. I had 29 bills plus some amendments passed in the seven-and-a-half years that I served in the legislature. That's very rare for any member who's not doing committee bills. Many of the ideas came from my constituents. I think it was the fact that I kept in constant communication with them that made the difference. I also believe that constant communication with my constituents went a long way toward eliminating opposition when I was up for reelection.

It was certainly a tough road, but when we were victorious on behalf of a citizen, my staff and I were very happy. When we were able to get something important passed, or we were able to break through bureaucracies to get people answers to their questions, we felt we were really making a difference. A lot of people, for example, were trying to get benefits from the VA for their ailing loved ones, and we were often able to intervene. One gentleman, years later, wrote me a testimonial because I was able to help his wife get her benefits, which enabled her life to be saved. I did these things not because I wanted accolades but because it was the right thing to do, and I also derived tremendous satisfaction from being able to help someone out.

My office had a standing order that carried through to when I was lieutenant governor: we were not to turn away anyone who called us for help. We'd always follow up to make sure the callers had received the help or information they needed. We may not have always provided the answer people wanted to hear, but we always provided an answer. My staff learned to expect that I'd follow up on these things. Maybe not that day or the next day—in fact it might be months later—but at some point, I'd say, "Remember Mr. Such-and-such who called the office? How did we resolve that?"

So there were ups and there were downs. I found some, if not many, political allies who shared similar views. One of them was former congressman Bill McCollum. He and I had similar issues with the Republican Party, especially regarding the lack of party support we'd received in our races. We met during the 2000 election, when I was running for Congress and he was running for the U.S. Senate. I got to know him and his wife, Ingrid, and we became friends. We approached elections in a similar way, especially since we lacked backing. We walked door to door. We waved signs. We stuffed envelopes. We were more part of our local parties than the national party. That's how we did things.

Prior to the 2010 election, Bill announced that he was running for governor, and I supported him. At the time, there was no one else running on the Republican side. But then Rick Scott came into the race, and the question was, who was Rick Scott?

Nobody in local politics really knew him. He was a private sector guy who'd been in the health-care business, which had made him a multimillionaire. But as the primary went on, I started to hear rumblings from folks around the state that he was going to win. Still, I was not about to jump ship and pull my support away from Bill just because he might not win. I'm the type of person who, once I've pledged my support, will maintain that support until my candidate releases me or drops out of the election campaign.

As it turned out, Rick Scott won. In August, not long after the primary, I received a phone call from Scott's campaign manager who told me that Scott wanted to meet with me to discuss joining him on the ticket. I was very reluctant because I didn't know him personally. We'd sat next to each other at an event once, but that was the extent of it. So my first question was, "Why me?"

"At least come talk to him," the campaign manager replied.

"If I'm on a list of 10, I'm not interested," I told her. "It's a waste of my time, and I'm not interested in meeting with him just because it would be good publicity for the campaign to say he's interviewing me."

"No, it's a very short list," she assured me.

"You know I didn't support Rick in the primary; I backed McCollum," I said.

She said they knew but still wanted to meet with me.

I kept pushing back because I had events lined up and my focus was on wrapping up my legislative term. I was the chair of the economic development council and I was working on a lot of issues. I'd seen that the state was spending less than 5 percent of its resources on economic development, and over 60 percent of its resources on education and health care. With the economy going south as it was, if we didn't do more to bring about jobs and grow the economy, we wouldn't have the money to fund education and health care. So there were a number of plans and initiatives that I wanted to launch when I came back into session the next time around.

But Scott's campaign manager was persistent. Finally, I said, "Okay, book the flight and I'll come." After hanging up, I immediately called my husband. He said, "Go ahead and talk with him and see what they're all about and if they're serious. Then we'll go from there."

I flew down to Miami. My appointment was supposed to be at 3:00 p.m. but was pushed to 4:00 p.m. Then 4:00 p.m. became 5:00 p.m. Apparently, Scott was interviewing somebody else before me, two other people as a matter of fact.

I'd made his campaign manager promise to have me be back in time to give a speech I had scheduled at the University of Florida, so I was thinking, "He'd better hurry up." Finally, after

5:00 p.m., I was called in by two of his attorneys. They'd reviewed my record and everything I'd submitted to them about my consulting clients and my franchise operations, the kind of work I'd done in the past, articles that had been written about me, and so on. They asked me all sorts of questions as part of their vetting process, and when they were comfortable with my responses, they introduced me to the candidate, Rick Scott.

He and I talked for a while. He told me about himself and where he grew up. I told him about my family, my time in the legislature, and my time in the military. It wasn't just cordial; I thought we actually hit it off. We talked about his private sector work and I shared with him the challenges I was facing on the economic development and transportation committees. His message was centered on jobs, and I was right there with him on that message.

He also admitted that he knew nothing about government and that he would like my help in creating legislation that would support his agenda of getting the state back to work. I said, "If you're looking for somebody to just be a bump on a log and do nothing, then I'm not your person."

"No, I want whoever's with me to be a workaholic like I am and to be engaged and work alongside with me on my agenda," he said. I told him I would welcome that if he ended up offering me the job.

He was late going to his next meeting because our conversation was flowing so easily. His attorney kept coming in to tell him he had to get to his next appointment, but he kept saying, "No, just a little while longer." Then, finally, he left, and I went to the airport to catch my flight.

On my way to the airport, he called and asked me if I would run with him. Even though our conversation had gone extremely well, I was in a state of disbelief. It was just so quick, and I was still thinking, "Why me?" So I asked him that.

"Why not you?" he replied.

I told him it just seemed so sudden. We barely knew each other.

"Don't you want to be on the ticket with me?" he asked.

"It's not that, but are you sure you don't want to think about it a little longer?"

"No, I would like you to run with me."

And that was that. I told him I'd talk to my family and we'd take it from there. It was another one of those moments, like winning my first election, when I think I should have been happy, clicking my heels like Dorothy, but it was just so surreal. It took a while to sink in, especially since I was still wondering why he had chosen me. He never gave me a real answer to that question. I wasn't one of the good old boys, and he was a millionaire with his own plane. Why me?

I called my husband and his exact words were, "Well, it's about time they (meaning the Republicans) recognized your worth."

Nolan understood. He'd heard, throughout the years, the party folks say, "Oh, she's a rising star. She's one of our up-and-comers," but it was just lip service. I never got the level of support from the party that others did. I was an outsider, and in his own way, Scott was too. He was new to Florida and not strongly connected to the local party or state party. That was one of the things that was appealing about him, because I knew the legislative process. I thought we might work well together as outsiders.

I called the kids, who said, "Go for it, Mom!" They never thought about themselves or about what having a mom in the spotlight would do to them. My youngest son, Necho, was 17 years old and just finishing high school. My daughter, Nyckie, was 21 years old and finishing college. And my eldest, Nolan, was playing NFL football for the Miami Dolphins. They've always been able to stay very grounded through all the ups and downs of my career, and that's helped me stay that way too.

Perhaps I should have seen it coming because of the fast and strange way it all began, but I never really felt completely part of the Scott campaign. For two-and-a-half months after that, I campaigned nonstop. I traveled all over with Scott's people, doing what was asked of me. My only stipulation was that when my son was playing football, I had to be either in front of a TV if it was an away game, or at the game if it was at home. Ever since my son had gone off to college and started playing football at the University of Maryland, we had been to all of his games. That's part of what we did as a family. When one of our kids had something going on, we had to be there. The campaign honored that.

Campaigning with someone you do not know is an odd situation because you're thrust together all of a sudden. Just the Scott family and I were on a bus, traveling to various places, and hopefully, getting to know each other. I thought he developed an appreciation for me and my work ethic during that time, but it was difficult to bond under the circumstances. And then there were things I started noticing that surprised me.

The state of Florida is very diverse. There's a large minority population that includes Hispanics, Blacks, and Asians, but the campaign staff made little effort to get into those communities. They allocated some money and hired a Hispanic to do outreach. They did some advertising on Hispanic radio and placed some ads on black radio at my urging. It was pretty superficial. One thing about me is that I hit a cross section of people. It's easy for me to go into the poorest neighborhoods or the most affluent or the most diverse, because I can relate to, and get along with, anybody.

I reached out to a well-regarded, experienced, black, political consultant named Clarence V. McKee and asked him to create an extensive outreach plan for reaching the Asian, Black, and Hispanic communities, and to submit it to Scott's campaign manager. He did, and the campaign manager loved it. The plan was then given to Scott's campaign consultant, who had worked with him for a number of years, and he said, "No, we're not going to do that." It was never really explained why, but the whole thing was just dropped. Maybe they assumed we didn't need those communities, but Scott was already having trouble capturing women voters and winning over past McCollum supporters. And yet we were doing very little to reach out to minorities, especially blacks.

So I had a conversation with Clarence, during which I said, "I still want to do direct outreach to these minority communities. If I'm successful, I will be the first black person elected statewide in Florida. First time. That's a big deal." As it turned out, I was the first woman and first black person elected as lieutenant governor in the state of Florida. How could I turn a blind eye to constituencies that I was a part of and that I would be making history for in the process?

The campaign didn't want it, but I did it anyway. Clarence coordinated the development of literature showcasing my work in the legislature that specifically impacted the minority community. Volunteers handed out this literature, and then I went out to churches and precinct areas in the Black, Asian, and Hispanic communities. I even went to a forum at Bishop Victor T. Curry's church in Miami that the campaign advised me not to go to because he was a Democrat. I was told it would be a "hostile environment" and that I shouldn't go because "they're going to be mean and we're not going to reap any benefits from it." But Bishop Curry has a charter school, a radio program, and one of the largest churches in the Miami inner city area. He's very influential, and on this particular night, even Al Sharpton attended the event.

It was one of the few times that I put my foot down. Even if I had to go by myself, I was going. And I did—just Clarence and I. I was the only Republican on the stage, but I won over so many people that night that even Al Sharpton called me to say they commended me for having the backbone (actually, he used a different word describing a part of the male anatomy) to show up. Besides that, our opponent didn't show. She assumed she had these people in the bag, so she didn't bother to come herself or send her running mate. And I pointed that out. I said, "I'm the only one here. I don't see the other side, and why would you want them if they're going to take you for granted? Every person who wants your vote ought to come and ask for it." The people gave me major props, even though the audience was almost all black Democrats.

Nobody from the Scott campaign realized what a difference events like that could make. Additionally, I reached out to the Jewish communities in Palm Beach County, which is traditionally Democrat. I met the acquaintance of a prominent Democratic operative in Palm Beach County who took a liking to me and offered to help. He suggested I conduct a robo-call to the Jewish communities in Broward and Palm Beach Counties the Saturday before the election, using the voice of a well-known Jewish ambassador. We obtained a list of over 80,000 phone numbers of Jewish voters and the voice of this ambassador asked all those voters to vote for Jennifer Carroll. When election day came, we couldn't declare victory that night. The race was just too tight. In the end, we won by 48.9 percent of the votes; the opponent got 47.7 percent. Had I not conducted the minority stealth campaign, which obtained 6 percent of black votes, Scott would have lost the election. Besides that, having me on the ticket helped with women, veterans, and minorities, not to mention McCollum voters who had known me for years.

When we won, I was happy of course, but I was already a little bit wary too. It hadn't been the smoothest campaign, but it was my hope that once the drama died down, we could really get good things done for the people.

CHAPTER 7

BEHIND CLOSED DOORS

"But Joseph said to them, 'Don't be afraid. Am I in the place of God? You intended to harm me, but God intended it for good to accomplish what is now being done, the saving of many lives.'"

—*Genesis 50:19–20*

The governor's birthday is December 1, so in the lull between the election and swearing-in in January, I sent him a birthday present. I remembered him stating on the campaign trail that he loved dark chocolate, so my husband and I sent him a big basket with all sorts of chocolates. I knew the basket was delivered, because I got a confirmation, but I never heard from him. Finally, I called him later in the day and asked, "Did you ever get something delivered from me?"

"Oh, yes," he said, "thank you." And that's how it was. During my entire time in office, I never received a birthday card or an anniversary card or anything that showed a personal touch.

That by itself wouldn't have been a big deal, but it was indicative of something. No matter what I did to try to establish a relationship with the governor, nothing worked. In the beginning, when I tried to set up a meeting or dinner with our spouses, his staff told me I had to go through the scheduling office to get an appointment. That was fine, I told myself. I'd play the game. But then they'd tell me he couldn't do this, he didn't have time for that. I was patient and jumped through the hoops, but when we'd finally meet, it just wasn't clicking.

Maybe he wanted it that way. Maybe that's just how he was with people. But it was not what I expected, based on our initial interview. Finally, I stopped trying to arrange any personal or social time with the governor, but I did continue to have weekly work meetings with him. And his chief of staff, at least the first two of them (he went through quite a few—four in less than two years) allowed me to attend staff meetings. Even though I had my own chief of staff, my schedule had to go through the governor's chief of staff for approval. That's how it was. The governor's staff ran the show.

The inauguration was a nice event in that all sorts of people, particularly minorities who may not have attended inaugurations before, spent their time and money to see this historic event since I was the first black woman elected to state office in Florida. Even people who were not Republicans and did not support Rick Scott came out.

That was touching to see, but during the inauguration, I was treated like an unwanted stepchild. It was all about Scott and his family, and I was left alone, unsure of what I was supposed to do or where I was supposed to go. That night at the ball I was even instructed not to go out into the crowd. They wanted the governor out there but asked me to stay in the wings. They never told me why, but I suspect it was because there were real dynamic differences between us in terms of our ability to speak and connect with people. I initially thought that was one of the ways I complemented him, but I think his staff was afraid he'd be upstaged.

The strange thing about being lieutenant governor is that there are no delineated duties. A statute states that the lieutenant governor is to be chairperson of Space Florida, but that's it. Any activities beyond that are activities the lieutenant governor has an interest in or the governor assigns.

At the outset the governor asked me to develop a portfolio of things I was interested in. I included in my portfolio trade/exports, military affairs, defense contracts, and of course, Space Florida. One of the governor's attorneys who had vetted me during the campaign wanted me to take over the Department of Business and Professional Regulations and the Department of Children and Families, but I explained that they were not areas of interest to me. I also pointed out that lieutenant governors don't usually run agencies. I wondered if they just wanted me on the ticket to win, and after that were trying to push me out of the position by making me an agency head. That way, the governor wouldn't have to deal with me regularly or have to share the spotlight.

I didn't realize until much later how close that intuition was to the truth. It wasn't until after I had left office that someone very high up in the governor's campaign told me that Governor Scott had not wanted a lieutenant governor in the first place. Of course, he never told me that. I would have turned down the position if he had.

Instead, I went to work on things we'd agreed would be in my portfolio. We had 20 military installations in the state and sequestration coming up. We needed to reinstitute the quarterly meetings that Jeb Bush used to have with our base commanders so they would have a connection with the executive office. We also had military defense contractors who were hurting for work. We needed to help those contractors position themselves to be awarded more contracts. We were also looking at issues with funding and strengthening our National Guard. The executive office didn't have much of a relationship with many parts of the military, so I fostered those relationships in Washington DC, and as a result, we were able to attract more missions in Florida, even though the military was consolidating or closing up shop in other areas.

Then, with Space Florida, we were looking at the end of the shuttle program, but we were able to get more commercial space missions coming to the cape. Despite what people were saying about the thousands of jobs that would be eliminated when the shuttle program ended, we were able, with the help of the economic development commission in the cape area, and the assistance of NASA Administrator Bolden and Bob Cabana, the executive director at NASA, to get many of those people re-employed with the new generation of space activities or in other places in the state.

Nobody in the administration could talk about those issues better than I could. Nobody worked harder to support those industries, and I kept the governor in the loop about all of it, whether his staff wanted me to or not.

When I was pregnant with my third born, I was a division officer in VP62. The person taking over my command didn't arrive until a week or two later than he was supposed to, so I was going into labor when he finally showed up. I saw it happen so often in the military: When people moved on to another job, the military didn't do enough to transition things properly and get the new people the information they needed. I was determined not to let that happen on my watch and to have a complete turnover with the lieutenant taking over my job. I had everything laid out: what my responsibilities were, what I had in the works, what I had completed, who did what. I had line items about each of these things for him to initial so it would all be official and on record. I was in labor while I went through everything with him. My husband was sitting in my office timing my contractions. The lieutenant was nervous and asked every so often, "Shouldn't you go to the hospital?" In between contractions, I told him, "Don't worry about it. We're going to finish this turnover today." And we did. Then my husband and I went to the hospital to deliver our son, Necho.

I was just as thorough with the governor. When they sent me on speaking engagements or I accomplished something with my portfolio items, I would always give the governor a briefing that included the information I'd gathered, what people were saying, what needed to be done, and so on. I would give him these briefings at our weekly meetings, the ones I had to keep scheduling because I couldn't get his staff to make them a standing order. I'd always get to the meetings on time, especially since his office was right down the hall. Then I'd have to sit and wait, because he'd be on the phone or one of his staffers would be in a discussion with him. My meetings were scheduled to last only one half hour, so the governor's conversations with others cut into our time, but finally, I'd get my turn. We'd chitchat about something he was involved in, and then I'd go into my spiel. It was brief, but I got to say what I needed to—that is, until his third chief of staff came into the picture, his third in less than a year. That's when I really started having problems in the office.

When Steve MacNamara took over as the governor's chief of staff, he wanted all information to be filtered through him. I felt I was there to support the governor and fully disclose to him any information that he might need to know, particularly anything that could pop up in the press. But when it got back to Steve that I was totally upfront with the governor, he'd say to me, "Why'd you tell the governor this?" Well, why not? The governor and I were elected, not his chief of staff and me. It was my responsibility to keep the governor informed. I don't think the governor ever truly appreciated my loyalty in this regard.

Because Steve couldn't stop me from speaking directly to the governor, it created a huge problem between us. He worked overtime to insert himself between me and the governor, and the governor let him. For example, in the first year, the governor invited me to sit with him when he interviewed people he was looking to appoint to commissions and boards. I knew a lot of people around the state from my time in the legislature, so I gave him my insights. When Steve came on board, he convinced the governor that it wasn't a good idea for me to sit in on those meetings, that only he and the governor should take part. "If she's there, it will make people think she's influencing you," he said. The governor bought that hook, line, and sinker.

After that, I had to have one of the governor's deputies with me anytime I met with someone. And I had to report back to the chief of staff what was said. I was also told I couldn't meet with lobbyists even though the governor's deputy directors, his chief of staff, and the governor himself all met with lobbyists.

When we got into office, it was clear that the governor wanted to be fiscally conservative. I was allotted six staff positions based on what previous lieutenant governors had had and I was informed about the salaries under the previous lieutenant governor. To do my part, I decided to come in a little under budget. Of course, I didn't know how much the governor was paying his people. Then the governor decided to put everybody's salaries on his website, and it turned out that my people were getting anywhere from $5,000 to $30,000 less than their counterparts on his staff. And because I had fewer staff members, they often had more to do.

My staff wanted to know why they were getting paid less, so I asked for a raise for them. I was able to get an increase for only two staff members. But even so, the incident opened up territory for Steve to exploit.

It began with my security. Again, previous lieutenant governors had spent far more on security and administration than I was spending. I was always very mindful of my spending and of making sure we accounted for every dollar. I even opted to stay at budget hotels with free breakfast and free Internet when I traveled, while the governor and his staff stayed at costly four-star hotels. When it came to my security, under FS 321.04 (3), the Florida Department of Highway Safety and Motor Vehicles assigned one patrol officer to the office of the governor. This officer had been designated by all other governors to be the protection officer for their lieutenant governors, all of whom were allowed to pick a specific security detail officer. And I did too, initially. But when my security detail officer had surgery on her shoulder, I had problems getting a replacement.

Steve saw it as an opportunity to do away with my security officer. I believe he was working on having state senators sponsor a bill that would do away with the lieutenant governor's position all together, and one way he planned to convince them was to show them how much money they could save. And the governor agreed with this plan. You'd think the man I ran with would stand up and say, "This is my lieutenant governor. I need her, and she needs protection," but no. All he would say when I protested this and other issues, was, "Oh, it's tough being a lieutenant governor."

The governor himself, on the other hand, employed three or four people for his and his wife's security. Finally, I asked to be given a budget for my security and agreed to work within that budget. So Steve tasked the deputy director, Mark Slager, and Julie Jones, the former director of the Florida Highway Patrol (FHP), to work with me on a budget. Julie Jones even admitted that I was very frugal, spending way less than previous lieutenant governors. As a matter of fact, even Steve commented that my spending was far less than recent lieutenant governors, especially Frank Brogan. But Julie's job was on the line and she played the game to give Steve what he wanted.

It took months to get that budget, but when I did, I went through it and realized that they had made the costs seem higher than they actually were by twice tabulating my security officer's salary. The security officer was not an additional employee whom they had to hire but, rather, somebody who had already been hired by the FHP, and whom the FHP assigned to me. The budget also specified that I could no longer select whomever I wanted as my security officer. Instead, the governor's staff would select that person, who had to be a trooper or a corporal, a lower rank than my previous security detail, who had been a captain. A Florida statute mandates that the security officers must have the rank of captain in order to gain the respect of staff who must cooperate with them in making security arrangements when the lieutenant governor travels. So Steve wanted to undermine the Florida statute, and he also wanted to limit my security to just a driver—someone who would only drop me off at my destination. This was at a time when I was being stalked and receiving threatening e-mails and phone calls. I was sent on a trade mission overseas without any security, and Manuel "Manny" Mencía, senior vice president of Enterprise Florida, was so frightened for my safety that he didn't want to have anything to do with any incident that might occur while the trade mission was underway. He couldn't believe the administration hadn't approved security for my overseas travel.

I finally went to Governor Scott and said, "Governor, my life is as important as yours, and my family values my safety just as much as yours does. Why would I, on behalf of the state, put myself in harm's way like this?"

This was around the time when Congresswoman Gabrielle Giffords was shot and I pointed that out to the governor as well. I said, "Would you want something like that to happen just to save just a little money?" The governor had no real response other than, "Oh, that issue is not taken care of yet." Even the one security officer I had wasn't enough to protect me from people who would come up to me, hug me, or surround me at events. Although that security officer did a fantastic job, he was overwhelmed and was greatly concerned for my safety. I'm just a huggable, touchable person, and I never stopped people from coming up close to me. But I knew it would feel very different if I were out there all on my own.

The attack on my security was just the beginning. Not long after, somebody new was hired as head of IT for the governor.

Now, this person was a friend of Steve's, which I didn't know, but I happened to remember that back in 2007, under then governor Charlie Crist, the guy had been fined over $61,000 for working as a state IT employee while also getting state contracts for his private company. I saw the press clip about the hiring of this guy when I was out of town. When I came back to the office, I told the governor what I knew about him, not suggesting that the governor fire him, only that he might want to be prepared in case the press asked him about it.

The governor appeared to not want to know about certain things, even if he were better off knowing them. He told Steve what I'd said and Steve pulled aside my chief of staff, John. He demanded to know why I'd given the governor this information. John didn't know what he was talking about. Steve said, "If she wants to undermine me, I can undermine with the best of them. If she knows what's good for her, she'll sit her a** in her office and do what she's told if she thinks she wants to be governor one day."

Now, give me a break. First, I didn't have my sights set on being governor. Second, who did he think he was to be saying such things about me to my own chief of staff?

He told John, "If you can't control her, I'll find someone who will," meaning he'd fire John and put somebody else in his spot. Fortunately, John was loyal enough to share this with me. Thinking that the governor would have my back, I didn't go to Steve. I went to Scott.

"Do you expect your chief of staff to be fully open and honest with you?" I asked him.

"Yes," the governor said.

"Then why would Steve expect my chief of staff to do anything less for me, and threaten him in this way?"

Again, the governor just gave me this song and dance: "Oh, it's tough being a lieutenant governor." That was his fallback line.

Of course, the governor told Steve what I had said, which made things worse for John and me. Steve did finally approach me and asked why I'd told the governor about the IT guy's past scandal. I said, "Why wouldn't I? I got elected with the governor and I work for the governor. I don't want him blindsided on my watch about something I could have warned him about."

"Well, next time, you come to me and let me know," he said.

"No, I'm going to the governor when I have things to share, and he can tell you if he wants to."

We left it at that.

My security problem went on for over six months. This was Steve's way of getting control, getting back at me, and letting me know who was boss. We were operating on a shoestring while Steve worked on my budget, yet I was still attending events. I worked out with Julie Jones that we could cut back on travel expenses if I traveled without security and then picked up security locally. They even stopped my aide from traveling with me, so I traveled alone.

I attended an event in Orlando, where I was given two local security staff because it was big event. However, Julie called in the middle of the event to remove one of them. After the event, people swarmed around me, talking and asking for my signature. I got to the door and my security officer said, "Wait here. I need to go get the car." So I was left standing there by myself. I was livid. My security officer was embarrassed and felt unprofessional because he knew if an incident occurred, he would be blamed, but there was nothing else he could do under the circumstances.

When I was on my own, after working hours, I didn't have security. I had security only for official events. The toying with my security was now the scuttlebutt at FHP districts throughout the state. Kevin Connor, a union member at FHP, called me. "It's not right what they're doing to you," he said. "They did not do this to any other lieutenant governor. Let me know if you need me to step up and raise voices for you." I told him not to because I was being a team player and not wanting to make the administration look bad.

My security staff in the Jacksonville area where I lived were livid too. To save costs, they had been instructed to just drop me off at my destination and not to do any advanced work. They said they would lose their badges before doing anything that would put my life in jeopardy. That's how professional they were. It was really an unfair position to put them in.

I kept bringing up to the governor that I didn't have a budget and was still in flux with my security. But he did little to intervene. Finally, they gave me a budget and our expenses were under it. As a matter of fact, the only time that we were over budget was the first year, and that was by only a couple of hundred bucks. Now, we were under budget by a couple of thousand.

There was no reason for any of it that I can see, except bullying. The governor used to say that he didn't like working for bullies. I shared that with my daughter once, and she said, "He doesn't like working for bullies, but he doesn't mind everybody else working for one."

At the time, I thought the denial of security for me was just a result of the usual power grabbing and manipulation that seems to go with politics. In hindsight, I wonder if it was the result of an orchestrated effort to get me to leave. A couple of reporters, particularly Steve Bousquet at the *Tampa Bay Times*, published articles suggesting I might not be on the ticket with the governor the next time around. When I read that, I asked the governor about it.

"Sure, you'll be on the ticket," he said. "Why wouldn't you be?"

I said, "I don't know, but just let me know."

It became clear over time that Steve's *modus operandi* was to create situations through which he would undermine or get rid of people who didn't go along with him. He did this with a number of secretaries and department heads whom the governor had appointed. For some reason, the governor trusted Steve and went along with his views of people.

A problem arose involving the Personal Injury Protection bill (PIP), which was the governor's priority bill in 2012. Steve and Chris Finkbeiner, who was the legislative affairs director, were running the show. They were going to bring the bill home for the governor and they wanted all the credit. But it came down to the eleventh hour. We were in the last day of session and the bill still hadn't passed.

The bill was not something I'd been asked to work on. I went to the senate floor that evening to say hi to some of my friends I'd served with in the legislature, but not to discuss PIP. Two members sought me out to have a more personal chat in the bubble, which is a back room where you can't be heard by people outside. They were interested in the space industry, which I was in charge of, so I let them know I would be in their area and that we could take the opportunity to look at a plan of action to increase our commercial space operation.

Afterward, I came back to my office to find a lot of hoopla from Chris. He had complained to Steve that I was influencing people on PIP. Some blogger had written that I was in the chamber, trying to get votes for the governor. Clearly, since I'd been talking in an area where the press couldn't have overheard me, this blogger had simply made assumptions. My chief of staff, in the meantime, had his butt chewed out by Chris for this, and Chris and Steve had already complained to the governor. At that moment, on the floor, Senator Latvala was holding the debate on PIP, and it was clear they didn't have enough votes. So they were probably looking for someone to blame.

Then the governor called me into his office to ask me not to interfere with what Chris and Steve were doing. He was already on their side even though he didn't have the facts and presumed my guilt without evidence. There I was, wondering why no one had simply asked me about the blog report instead of blindly believing it. I told the governor I hadn't had a conversation about PIP with anyone, to which he replied, "Oh, you know how people perceive things."

I was so upset with the governor. I couldn't believe he was taking their side, even after they'd made false assumptions. As it turned out, they eventually had to ask me for my help. The PIP bill was going down, and they were short a couple of votes. They asked me to persuade my friends from the legislature to support the bill.

I probably should have said, "Screw y'all," but being a team player, I did them the favor. I talked to some people and got the needed support. The bill passed by one vote. When I came back from the floor that time, I was everybody's hero, but I wanted to smack them. It was another example of a time in my life when I should have been celebrating something I had accomplished, but I couldn't appreciate the moment because of the way I'd been treated. They had been so afraid I'd sabotage the bill, and then, they couldn't get the doggone thing passed on their own.

After that, it seemed to be one thing after another with Steve. There was an incident with Paige Kreegel, who was a friend and someone I'd worked with for many years in the Florida House of Representatives. Paige was running for Congress and asked me to endorse him, but the governor didn't want me to give any endorsements in the primaries. Paige said, "Ask him anyhow because I can't see him saying no since I raised money for his campaign." So I did.

He was running in the primary against former congressman Trey Radel, who was later busted for buying drugs and had to leave office. I didn't know this at the time and the governor should have been honest with me, but the governor, according to Trey's bragging, was a supporter of his. Still, I got the governor's blessing to endorse Paige Kreegel.

I wrote the endorsement letter, sent it to Paige, and Paige put it in the papers. Then Steve told the governor I shouldn't be endorsing anyone if the governor wasn't publicly endorsing anyone. So the governor asked me to pull my endorsement.

If he had just said, from the start, "Listen, I'm quietly supporting Trey," I would have been fine with that. The way the situation was handled just made the governor appear to be unable to make decisions by himself, and pulling my endorsement made me come across as wishy-washy.

In another incident, Scott Walker, the governor of Wisconsin, was coming to Florida as part of a tour to raise money for his recall election. At a National Lieutenant Governors Association meeting, Rebecca Kleefisch, Wisconsin's lieutenant governor, talked to us about how she too had to raise money. In a regular election, the governor and lieutenant governor run on the same ticket together, but because this was a special recall election, she had to run a separate campaign, and she didn't have much money to work with.

I decided to help her with fundraising, along with a couple of other lieutenant governors. I went to Governor Scott, shared the story, and asked him if it was okay to organize some fundraisers for Rebecca. He said yes. We sat face-to-face in the office, and he said yes.

So I moved forward. I had set up three fundraisers within a week when Steve advised the governor I shouldn't be doing fundraisers. The governor told me that any money raised inside the state should be going to our campaign, not to an external cause, and he asked me to stop organizing further fundraisers. First, individuals are limited by law in how much money they can donate. So, if they're willing to give more than their maximum, why shouldn't the surplus go to a party member in another state? Second, candidates from other states regularly hold fundraisers in our state, so how does it help if we don't participate? Third, if the recall election had been successful, Florida could have been the next place where the opposition would try this tactic. The rationale to not help just didn't make sense.

I think they realized that since Governor Scott wasn't doing much to help Governor Walker, my setting up three fundraisers for Governor Walker's lieutenant governor could make Scott look bad. So now, the governor asked me to cancel the fundraisers— only a week before they were due to take place.

Being a team player, I cancelled them. It turned out Rebecca had been worried about attending the Florida fundraisers because they would have been held during the Wisconsin primary election, which she would have missed. She was facing opposition in her primary election, and had she lost, Governor Walker could have ended up sharing his office with a member of a different party.

The work environment in Governor Scott's administration reminded me, at times, of the male-dominated environment of the military. It was a boy's club. Although I was elected second in command, when the establishment GOPers mentioned the names of those who might be governor after Scott, they never mentioned mine. The list was always of good old boys. What was so interesting was that they would say this in front of me and never saw how dismissive they were being. They weren't aware of their exclusiveness, or they just didn't care.

The press reported that Steve might have engaged in unethical behavior in government contracting while working for the state senate. Still, the governor defended him in the press. Continuing the good old boy behavior, Governor Scott allowed Steve to determine his own timeframe for leaving and to go with a severance.

When Adam Hollingsworth, the new chief of staff, came in, I had an opportunity to sit down and explain to him what my staff and I had been through under Steve. Just as I had back in my military days, I'd kept notes on everything. Adam was from Jacksonville and had worked on the campaign, so I knew him a little, or so I thought. I later learned that Adam worked for my Democrat opponent, Congresswoman Corrine Brown, and he was also a financial contributor to her campaign.

I was hoping things would get better under his leadership, but Adam turned out to be even more ruthless than Steve had been. It might have been different if I'd had a better relationship with the governor or if the governor valued me, but as I mentioned, I was never able to form any kind of bond with him.

I attended an Epiphany celebration at a Greek festival one day. It was a very long event in a very hot church. I started feeling faint and went to the restroom, where I blacked out and fell, hitting my head on the concrete floor. I'd never blacked out before. I called the governor and left him a message about what had happened, but he never called back.

In a conversation a couple of weeks later, we were talking about the event and I mentioned my blackout. The governor said, "Oh, you hit your head? Okay." And that was the end of that. This is someone who came from the health-care industry and that's all he had to say? Clearly, something was missing there, some ability to make personal connections that he just didn't have.

I think the governor assumed his political position would be similar to his private sector position, in which he was CEO, the top dog, and everybody else had to do what he wanted. But at the end of the day, that's not how government—in which a variety of different people have been elected by the citizens—works. I think his staff picked up on this about him and tried to exploit it for their own gain. They rallied around him to make him feel he was king, and in doing so, they solidified their own power positions.

I, on the other hand, come from a military environment where there's a commanding officer and an executive officer who is there to support the commanding officer. That's how I always saw my role and why, I think, I tolerated as much bad treatment as I did. I thought the roles were clear, and I wasn't looking to grab power or claim credit. I just thought I was supposed to do my best to support the governor, not watch my back. But that was probably a mistake. Early on, after taking office, the communications department had a standing order to be wing clippers. They were to minimize any good press about me so I wouldn't be too visible or upstage the governor. Even the folks in communications thought this was perplexing. Considering my legislative experience and relationships with members in the Florida House of Representatives and Senate, I never understood the unwillingness of the governor to use me to my full capacity.

But I always put on a good face for the public and the press, so very little of this was seen on the outside, though some people picked up signs. I'm a very good public speaker and I did a lot of public speaking during the campaign, but the governor wasn't great at it. Probably to minimize the contrast between us, the staff reduced my speaking engagements, particularly when the governor and I attended events together. That didn't go unnoticed. People started asking why I wasn't getting out there more, why the governor wasn't using me more. I would just say, "Oh, he's very supportive of me," and smile. In the military, you're taught to be a team player, so that's how I was, always, even as my hair was falling out from all the stress I was under.

CHAPTER 8

BETRAYAL AND LEAVING OFFICE

"God will never leave you or forsake you."

—*Joshua 1:15*

When Adam came in as chief of staff, he said they wanted to get me more involved in the governor's work, including the next campaign. But that never materialized. My hopes that things would get better under him didn't last long.

I think the decision had been made, long before, that I wouldn't be on the ticket the next time around, and they just had to figure out a way to make that happen. As I mentioned earlier, reports had already appeared in the press, including articles by reporters with connections to Steve McNamara. I don't think those reporters just came up with the idea on their own. Many times the media beast was fed by people within the administration.

The contentious environment was hard on my staff too. If I was being chewed out, left out of the loop, or disrespected, so were they. My staff and I held weekly devotionals in the office to keep our spirits up and keep us sane. Everyone participated, with the exception of one staffer, Carletha Lamons-Cole. She was a self-professed ordained minister, but she never wanted to participate. I thought that was odd (and would remember it later when things started to go downhill with her), but at that time I felt that was fine if that was how she felt.

We also had regular dinners and lunches together and celebrated birthdays and holidays. I gave flowers and balloons to all the mothers on my staff, including Carletha, for Mother's Day, and bought all my staff Christmas presents. When I went on overseas trips, I always brought back trinkets for everyone. And then, of course, our constituents kept us going. Just as when I served in the legislature, my staff had standing orders to keep a record of any question or request from anyone who called the office. Those connections we made with the people we served were gratifying, even in the midst of everything else.

It became clear pretty quickly that Adam was not planning to include me any more than Steve had. Decisions were made without my input, and he'd show up at my office to tell me what the talking points had been. I would sometimes point out that the new talking points were different from what the governor had campaigned on. For example, when we came into office, the governor said the unemployment rate was 12 percent. Six months later, the talking points changed that number to 11.4 percent. I pointed out to Adam that if they wanted me out there, selling these talking points, I needed to understand why things had changed.

He said, "Oh yes, that's my fault. I'll have you included more." It never happened.

In fact, Adam was so confident in his position that he felt comfortable instructing me on how to dress. I was known as one of the best-dressed women in Tallahassee. One day, when I had no office meetings, only a night function at the governor's mansion, I wore Vince Camuto pants and a blouse with Michael Kors five-inch boots. This was not something Adam approved of and he made sure he shared that with me. He ordered me not to wear the outfit to the mansion that evening. Although I had a change of clothing for the night function, I thought it very presumptuous of him to chastise me in this manner.

Then, in August 2012, our state hosted the Republican National Convention (RNC) in Tampa that kicked off Mitt Romney's presidential run. The big news at the time was that a tropical storm had impacted Haiti and was coming up the coast. The governor was slated to speak Monday and Ann Romney on Tuesday. But Ann Romney canceled because of the storm.

Adam felt the governor had been given one of the worst times to speak at the convention, on a night that wasn't going to be covered in the national press. So once they found out Ann Romney wasn't speaking, they figured they too could use the storm as an excuse to bow out so the governor could avoid looking as if he just didn't want to do it.

People started coming in on Saturday, and I had all sorts of events scheduled with officials and delegates from other states. We were the host state, so I wanted to accept as many invitations as I could. Despite this, Adam cancelled all my events and directed me not to do anything, reasoning that if the governor wasn't going to be active, I couldn't be either. Otherwise, people would ask questions. I had to sit in my hotel room with nothing to do for two days. My birthday is August 27 and some people had been planning for months to throw me a party. I even had to cancel my birthday party at Adam's order. It was just so silly.

The storm passed through without much consequence. There was some flooding in places, but nothing that wouldn't have happened during normal rainfall.

On the last day, Thursday, when Mitt Romney was to give his speech, Adam finally allowed the governor to come to the convention. They had planned a fundraiser in a suite above the convention floor, and I was directed to entertain the guests until the governor arrived.

Since this was our state and we were the hosts, I had already been down on the floor and met the other delegations. But the governor hadn't been on the floor all week. So when he arrived, I asked his staff, "Is the governor going to the floor?" His communications people said, "No. We've been instructed by Adam to have him stay in the suite." I said, "Now, think of the optics here. The governor hasn't been here all week. The RNC is being hosted in his state and he isn't even going to take the opportunity to meet the other states' delegations or at least thank them for coming to his state?"

"Well, that's what we've been instructed," they said.

They were all afraid to go against Adam. I spoke with three different communications staffers, and none of them wanted to touch it. They said, "You talk to the governor."

So I took the governor aside and told him my concerns about how it might look if, on the night of Romney's big speech, he didn't even make an appearance on the floor in his own state. He thought about it for a couple of minutes and then announced, "I'm going down to the floor."

Lo and behold, the next day, the newspapers made a comment about the governor finally showing up on the floor. Had he not done it, it could have been a much bigger story. Someone might have interpreted it as a slight against Romney. Some news stories had already come out mentioning the fact that Romney had been campaigning in the state leading up the convention and that the governor had participated in few of those events. Even after everything that had happened, I still felt it was my job to look out for the governor. Another instance of standing up for Governor Scott was when Senator Gaetz personally attacked me in the press after I defended Governor Scott against Gaetz' claim that Scott was going to cut funding from the Florida Defense Support Task Force. The governor did not come to my defense, this time or any other time I came under attack. Yet I maintained my loyalty.

It all started to take its toll on me. I wasn't exaggerating when I said my hair was falling out. It was coming out in clumps. The strain was such that I quietly started looking at my options for transitioning out of office. I contracted with someone to update my resume, and I was even approached by folks in Washington DC about an ambassadorial position in Trinidad, which would have been a dream job.

My chief of staff, John, was one of the few people I confided in about this. Knowing that I might not be in office much longer, he told me he had an interview for another position. I encouraged him, saying, "Who knows what's going to happen with the reelection, so you might as well make your way now."

I kept this all very quiet. Besides John, I told one former staffer of the governor who had been asked to resign for no reason, and another former senior staffer. I don't think anyone in the governor's office knew I was looking at other options, but secrets are hard to keep in politics. Perhaps word got back that I was talking to somebody in Washington or something like that. If so, I'm sure it would have angered them. Maybe they didn't know it, but they were already planning to get rid of me. Whatever the case, the Allied Veterans scandal took me by surprise, or at least, it surprised me that anyone could believe I was somehow involved in it.

Allied Veterans had been a client of mine back in 2009 and 2010, when I had a public relations consulting and franchise business during my time in the legislature. My work was as an independent consultant to give public relations strategies, not an employee or officer with the charity. I didn't have anything to do with running its organization or handling its finances. My contract with that organization was totally limited to public relations. Mine was one of several PR firms giving the charity guidance on how to best communicate with the public and elected officials. Of course, this work was disclosed to the governor's team along with all my other past work when they first vetted me.

Allied Veterans was a charity organization that raised money for veterans' causes and operated under a Florida statute. The organization had been a well-known entity for a while, one that the governor himself took financial contributions from, as did Florida Attorney General Pam Bondi ($25,000), Florida Speaker of the House who opposed gaming, Dean Cannon ($25,000), and the Republican Party of Florida ($300,000), among others. There were lots of lobbyists, including former mayors, former city council members, and legislators, who were actively lobbying for, and were paid by, Allied Veterans. In fact, in 2009 I saw a video in which Congressman Ander Crenshaw praised the organization for stepping up to contribute over $1.8 million to veterans' organizations. His words were something to the effect that government can't do everything and Allied Veterans has stepped up to do what government was not doing. On the outside, Allied Veterans appeared to be doing good things. How I and no one else in politics became tied to the scandal is mysterious.

If the governor had just asked me to leave, I would have left. As I've often discussed in these pages, in the military, when your superior officer asks you to step aside, you follow that order. I would have done it gladly at that point, since the job wasn't exactly working out well for me. But I think he and his staff were worried that if they asked the first black woman elected to the office to leave, they would not look good.

So they had to find a cover story. When the governor took office in 2011, the Florida Department of Law Enforcement (FDLE) worked for him and would have briefed him on big investigations that the FBI was doing in the state. So he would have known about the FBI's investigation into Allied Veterans.

Now, the FBI had been investigating Allied Veterans since 2007, long before we came into office. Allied Veterans' Internet cafes received registration to operate from the Florida Commissioner of Agriculture, under Florida Statue 849.0931, and Florida law gives no guidelines on how much a charitable organization should spend on its own operations. The FBI investigation had something to do with illegal gambling, since people could buy Internet time at the cafes and, in the process, were given an opportunity to see if they might win something.

Around this time, it became known that the FBI was planning to arrest some folks at Allied Veterans, and since my company had carried out PR work for the charity years before, someone must have decided it would be a good idea to link me to the allegations as a way of asking me to leave office. The FBI was not investigating me or my company. I was not questioned about my work with Allied Veterans, let alone charged with anything. In my mind, there was no link between me and any allegations against Allied Veterans, so how would I ever have seen it coming?

One day, I was in my office when two FDLE officers came in to talk to me. Now remember, the FDLE works for the governor, they were not the federal agency investigating Allied Veterans. That was the FBI. The FDLE officers asked me basic questions and informed me that some members of Allied Veterans were about to be arrested. I don't think the exchange lasted even 30 minutes. Then they left my office, at which time the governor's chief of staff, Adam, and his general counsel, who were waiting outside my office, immediately walked in. I didn't link the two events at the time.

They wanted to know what the FDLE had said to me, so I shared the conversation with them, which seemed pretty innocuous to me. I had been planning to continue with my day since I had a full schedule and I was expecting visitors. It was then that they dropped the bomb.

"Well, we spoke with the governor a couple days ago, and he would like for you to resign."

"Why?" I asked.

"The governor wants to be focused on his legislative agenda and he doesn't want any distractions."

They had my resignation letter already typed. It was just a one-liner saying I was leaving. They passed it to me and I signed it. "Fine," I thought, "if this guy doesn't want me here, then I'll go. I've had enough." It was a knee-jerk reaction. It was so demoralizing and disrespectful for Governor Scott to send a subordinate to fire me.

It all happened so fast and was such a surprise that I really didn't take enough time to think about it. As soon as I had signed the paper, they said, "Cancel all your appointments and the governor will hold a press conference tomorrow. Stay in the office and don't speak to anyone. We'll come back at 3:00 p.m. to talk to you about how the press conference is going to go."

After that, I basically sat there all day waiting for them to come back. I told my assistant to cancel everything. I told my chief of staff what I'd agreed to do and, right away, he said, "You should have fought."

"It doesn't matter," I said. "I wanted to leave anyway, so it's no big deal."

"No big deal?" he said. "You know how it's going to look?"

"Why?" I asked. "I didn't do anything wrong." I still didn't see it coming.

Besides that, I told my husband and the kids, and I called the Dolphins, my son's team, to make them aware in case any press approached him about it. That was it. The rest of the day, I just sat there. Then, I heard my chief of staff was chewed out for not making me stay in my office. Apparently, another whisper campaign had made its way around the office, spreading the suggestion that I was going to hold a press conference of my own.

John came in to tell me about the press conference rumors, and I just said, "Gee whiz, what's wrong with these people?" Of course, at the time I didn't realize how afraid they were that I'd do just that. Because if I had held a press conference, it would have upset the narrative that they had carefully planned for the following day when the governor held his press conference.

The governor wasn't even in that day. In fact, we never talked again. At 3:00 p.m., Adam and the governor's general counsel came back. I asked them, "By the way, when is my resignation effective?" They said, "Today." I was already off the clock as far as salary and benefits were concerned.

Steve McNamara, when he left under the cloud of alleged wrongdoing, was given months to transition out and severance pay on top of it. Here I was, cut off, and I hadn't done anything wrong. I didn't even have a briefing with the human resources staff. Adam gave me a typed piece of paper that basically asked me to turn in my phone and anything that belonged to the office, and provided a phone number to call if I had questions about my health benefits. That was it. Adam pulled a face as if to say, "Oh, sorry about this," and walked out.

After that, I packed up my goods and went home. My security officer was very sympathetic and such a good guy. Normally, because I lived two-and-a-half hours from Tallahassee, he would drop me off at a halfway point and then the Jacksonville people would pick me up and take me home. But he felt so bad for me that he took me all the way home and drove back to Tallahassee.

When I arrived at home that night, I didn't feel anything but relief. I was finally free. I didn't have anybody to tell me what to do, where to go, who I could talk to, or what I could say. I didn't have anyone stabbing me in the back or watching over me all the time. I really thought I was free.

CHAPTER 9

MEDIA MATTERS AND MALPRACTICE

*"You shall not bear false witness
against your neighbor. "*

—*Exodus 20:16*

I didn't feel much of anything until the next day when the press conference was held. I was home alone when I watched it on television. I'd been told the governor was going to say that in order to avoid being a distraction to him and his legislative agenda, I had resigned. But that's not exactly what he said.

What the governor said was that after I spoke to the FDLE, I resigned. Until then, those had been two separate events in my mind. He left out the fact that I was *asked* to resign and that his people were waiting outside my office after the FDLE left to deliver his request for my resignation. He did not mention the fact that there were no charges or even an investigation underway that suggested I had done anything wrong.

I suddenly saw how bad this looked, and I was knocked to my knees. What he said wasn't a lie, exactly, but it certainly gave the impression I had resigned *because* of the Allied Veterans investigation, which was far from the truth. I firmly believe the governor's people staged the whole incident so they could frame the narrative in just this way. I believe they asked FDLE staff to talk to me about the Allied Veterans affair, which explains why our conversation was so strange. I'm sure it was no coincidence that Adam and the governor's general counsel were waiting to ambush me right after the FDLE staff left. That's how they were able to link the two events.

The media, not surprisingly, picked up the story and reported it just the way the governor framed it. "Lt. Gov. Jennifer Carroll resigns amid state, federal probe of nonprofit veterans group," the *Miami Herald* headline read. "Florida Lt. Gov. Jennifer Carroll resigns over Internet gambling scandal," a blogger reported. Nobody questioned the facts, nobody looked into the details, and the governor's narrative went out in the press all over the world.

I just kept telling myself that people would realize, once they looked into it, that if any wrongdoing had occurred at Allied Veterans, I had nothing to do with it, no more than had any of the other many politicians—including the governor himself—who had taken money from the charity or were connected to it in some other way over the years. I still thought the truth mattered.

On the one hand, I was furious, but on the other, I was deeply hurt. I didn't want to see people right away or face the public. But, of course, the press was calling, so I contacted a PR firm in Tallahassee. Rick Oppenheimer became my spokesperson. He was sympathetic. I shared with him the whole story and he was 100 percent behind me. I wondered why I hadn't received this kind of support from Governor Scott. As a former lawyer, Governor Scott should have understood the U.S. Constitution and its provision of due process for citizens, which he did not provide to me.

Rick reached out to the press and I made a statement. I talked about not wanting to be a distraction for the governor and not wanting to put pressure on my family. I didn't say that he asked me to resign. I was angry, and I'm not sure why I didn't let more of my anger out at that point. I guess I was still covering for him and for the Republican Party. I was still being the team player I'd always been. But the more I thought about it, the more I thought, "Forget that. I'm going to tell my side of the story." Rick coordinated an interview for me the following week with what turned out to be a pretty fair Associated Press reporter named Brandon Farrington, out of Tallahassee.

Even in that interview, I still covered to a degree, but I did explain exactly how the circumstances had played out and how they had asked me to resign. But when Brandon asked me, "How did it make you feel?" and I wanted to explode, I didn't. I decided to keep calm and not make a big deal about it.

"You know what? It's his ticket," I said. "He didn't want me on it, so I honored his wishes."

Then Brandon asked again, "How did it make you feel?" "Pissed" is what I wanted to say. I felt as an unsuspecting Nancy Kerrigan must have when she was whacked in the knees by her own teammate. I felt as I had when my aunt took my father away without telling me. I felt betrayed, but I didn't say so. I kept my cool. However, I did tell Brandon what really happened and it was the first time the public had heard the details.

After that, Leslie Dougher, chairperson of the Clay Republican Executive Committee, called me to let me know she was there for me. "We need to get your story out," she said, and she coordinated with a TV station in Jacksonville to have me appear on the Kent Justice show. Still, the real details of what happened weren't as widely reported as the story that I had resigned amid scandal. But at least they were out there.

The media reached out to some former colleagues in Tallahassee for comments, but none of them said anything negative, with the exception of two people. Without knowing any details, Senator Gaetz said, "When you deal with bad people and you make bad decisions, these bad things happen." Also, a former House of Representatives member commented on my guilt. I was so surprised by that because I'd helped him a great deal when he entered the Florida legislature. I had held his hand and made sure he understood how things worked. He was among a group of members who used to call me "den mom" because I tried to make sure they assimilated well. But he just leaped to the assumption that I'd done something wrong, rather than saying, "We don't know what has occurred but we're going to miss her," or something to that effect. It was disheartening.

What was heartening was the support I received from a number of people who reached out to me. They included Bea Thomas, a good supporter in the Pensacola area, and Sandy Aguilar, who ran a program for displaced women that I supported. Sandy and my sister, Cheryl, my biological mother's daughter, fasted for days with me, in prayer. My friend Art called me and just listened while I told him how hurt and depressed I was. And then he told me, "Pick your head up and go out and show your face to the world. You did nothing wrong, so all the forces of darkness cannot keep you from where God wants you to go." That was a wake-up call that I really needed to snap out of my depression because God wouldn't put me through something that he wouldn't help me out of. With every burden, there is a blessing.

Another person, Willie Miller Jr., whom I didn't even recall meeting, e-mailed me a 31-day devotional with a quote from Leslie Barner that read, "When life turns you upside down, you learn how to turn to God." I read that daily and I got on my knees and prayed. Part of the devotional asks you to write down your requests to God, so I started writing requests every day. Then, some days, I went without a request and I just thanked God for loving me.

My staff members were given positions in other areas of government—they were state employees, so the governor's administration had to do that for them—except for John, who left for the private sector, and one other staff member named Phyllis, who had worked for the past three lieutenant governors. I used to call her Mom because she treated me as if I were her daughter. She was a former Marine and a tough old cookie. She had worked in constituent services for years, dealing with people who called the office, usually with complaints. She was very good with them, handling even the most irate person with grace and care. She was so upset by what had happened that she didn't want anything to do with the administration after that and she left her job.

My husband was furious, of course. He and my children knew how much work and how many hours I'd put in and how committed I'd been to the governor. My youngest son still doesn't want to see anyone who looks like Rick Scott. My son Necho said, "No decent, self-respecting man with integrity would want to see his mother, sister, wife, or daughter being treated with that kind of maliciousness and not react to defend her." All my kids were hurt by how their mother was treated, and I had to put on a brave face because I didn't want what was happening to me to overtake their lives.

A lot of people have asked why I didn't do more to fight. It's hard to make people understand what was going on behind closed doors and for how long it had been going on. I was so tired of it all by then. The guy in charge didn't want me there, so why would I stay? If I had, they probably would have had me just sit at my desk and twiddle my thumbs until the term ran out. I was already unhappy and that would have made me miserable.

So I thought, "Fine, I'll leave now. I'll hurry up and get my civilian life started so I can escape all this BS and spend time with my family." It felt overwhelming because it was not just about taking on the governor. It was about taking on the media as well.

It amazes me how bullying and careless the media can be sometimes. It seems to me that if someone is accused of something, before reporting it, the media should stop and say, "Wait a minute. What's the basis of this claim?" But so often, their interests lie in sensationalism rather than truth telling. They'd rather tell the quick story with the attention-grabbing headline than do the work of peeling back the onion to find the whole truth. Too often, they're more interested in inciting emotion than reporting facts. And readers don't have the time or interest to question what they read. They don't usually stop to ask, "Is this factual enough? Let me get the rest of the story."

I mentioned earlier that when I was in office I had a staff member named Carletha Cole. I met her when she was the chairperson of the Suburban Republican Women's Club. She was also a member of the African American Leadership Council, which I chaired, and she'd helped me out on the gubernatorial campaign. When I began my work as lieutenant governor, I was looking to hire a communications person, and after my first choice was unable to take the job, I thought of Carletha. She seemed to be a good candidate because she had her own PR consulting business, was not fully employed, and had created promotional materials for the African American Republican Leadership Council created by Chairman Jim Greer.

I try to be very fair with my employees. I'm not a knee-jerk person who fires people as soon as they do something wrong. I counsel them and give them constructive criticism. I lay out a plan describing what improvement I expect from them. If they don't show improvement, we part ways.

Shortly after I took up my new position, Carletha decided she wanted to be my travel aide. Her work was mostly done in the office, but she wanted to be in the public eye. I already had a travel aide and told her, "That's not your job."

That was fine at first, but later, she started having trouble with other office staff. She and my executive secretary, Patti, had arguments. In the meantime, she offered to create a website for me. The governor's chief of staff had not wanted me to have a website. This was another one of those wing-clipper situations. All other lieutenant governors had websites, but that seemed to be beside the point. Still, I felt I needed to let people know what I was working on. Otherwise, my silence could have given them more fodder for their claim that the job was worthless and lieutenant governor didn't do anything except wait for the governor to die. So I pushed for the website, and the governor's staff finally said I could have one, but they weren't going to pay for it.

My chief of staff, John, would send me samples of the website in progress when I was on the road, and I'd send back corrections. I really wanted to launch the website, but it was delayed several times. When I asked John what was going on, he said, "Carletha says she has to do it when she gets off work." I asked why she couldn't work on it at the office and he started putting the pressure on her to get the work done at the office. What we thought was happening was that despite what she told us, she didn't really know how to create websites, so she was getting someone to do it on the side. That's why she only wanted to work on it outside the office.

Around that time, she started recording John. One day I was about to leave for a trip when John came into my office. "Ma'am," he said, "Carletha is making more problems in the office for us. Between everything else I'm doing, this is just too much babysitting."

While I was out of the office, a fax came in. It concerned a project Carletha was working on. Patti, my executive secretary saw it, and because Carletha wasn't there, she took it upon herself to reply to it. When Carletha found out, she took offense and yelled at Patti, "If you want to do my work, just do it all yourself!"

So that day, I sat down with John, Patti, and Carletha to hash things out. I said, "Listen, we're all adults here. We have a small staff. We should be working together as a family. If we have problems, let's talk it out with one another. We have citizens out there whom we need to assist and that's where our focus needs to be."

Then I said, "From here on out, we start with a clean slate. Everybody on board?" Everybody agreed.

The next day, Carletha called the press to leak the information that we had "dysfunction in the lieutenant governor's office that was stopping the lieutenant governor and governor from doing their work, and this was the job of a lifetime for her." Steve found out and had her fired. A few days after that, she started calling reporters to offer them tapes she had secretly recorded of John.

Now, in the state of Florida, it's a felony to record people without their permission. And besides that, I firmly believe that her recordings were altered. Eventually, she released them to the press, probably in an effort to get John fired. In them, his voice is clear but hers comes across as very garbled. For example, you can clearly hear him saying, "The governor is not leading . . ." and then the recording cuts off and you can't hear Carletha. Then John says, "He's afraid of her," referring to Steve MacNamara being afraid of me. It was a very short tape with just little snippets of things like that.

A lot of reporters didn't touch the story because they weren't able to verify the authenticity of the tapes. However, one reporter in Jacksonville, Matt Dixon, who hated my guts and never printed a good story about me, took the story and released the tape. About a month later, Carletha was arrested for illegally wiretapping my chief of staff.

Now, the case was really between Carletha and my chief of staff, John, since he was the only one she recorded. But Carletha hired an attorney in Tallahassee named Steven Andrews who, during the Republican primary, had served the governor with papers to disclose a deposition he'd given while at Hospital Corporation of America (HCA). The governor had to pay the largest fine in history for Medicare fraud when he was president of HCA, and that came out because of what Andrews had done. They had some additional run-ins over a property dispute and some work Andrews had been contracted to do by the Florida Republican Party. He had an axe to grind with the governor, I was collateral damage, and he was the attorney she got to defend her in her illegal wiretapping case.

Andrews knew it would be hard for me to file a defamation of character lawsuit based on any information brought out in court that was then picked up by the press, no matter how inaccurate it was or how widely it was reported. The media also knew I was muted and was not allowed by the administration to defend myself. It is next to impossible for elected officials to win a defamation case. To win a defamation case, you have to show actual malice on the part of the person making the statement, and if the information comes out during a court case, malice is hard to prove. So they used Carletha's illegal wiretapping case to suck me into it and set the stage to elicit money for a wrongful termination case they planned to bring. Carletha's first tactic was to make up stories to suggest racism, a hostile working environment, and—her final straw—to claim retaliation was the reason she'd been fired, rather than for violating her contract by going to the press.

To set up the scenario for her claim of retaliation, Carletha took a polygraph test, during which she said she had found me and my female travel aide in a compromising position. The polygraph results stated, "heavy breathing, hard to read, but she passes." It was a ridiculous charge that didn't have anything to do with the felony case she was facing, but Andrews tried to have her polygraph admitted in court as a way of injecting me into the case to later sue the state for back pay. Meanwhile, I was not a party in the case so I couldn't defend myself in court. And I couldn't sue her for defamation because of the way the information came out. She never publicly made the claim, nor did her attorney on her behalf. It seemed so clear that it was all just a maneuver on the part of Carletha and her lawyer. She was looking at a five-year prison sentence and having a felony charge on her record, so she had nothing to lose. When Steven Andrews submitted this in court, the judge said, "Why is this even relevant?" Additionally, polygraphs aren't admissible as court evidence because the best liars can pass them. So the judge ruled her polygraph inadmissible.

The judge then ordered the item sealed, but Gary Fineout, an Associated Press reporter, went to the clerk's office in Tallahassee and somehow obtained this information. He then called the governor's communication staff member, Brian Burgess, to say, "Oh, Brian, I guess I wasn't supposed to get this information, but I got it by accident. And I'm going to press with it. Do you have a comment?"

And so the "news" morphed from "compromising position," to "I was having a lesbian affair" with someone who worked for me. No attempt was made to verify the claim. It was just a news story that, because Fineout was an Associated Press reporter, was picked up nationally and internationally.

Adam Hollingsworth had taken over as chief of staff by then and he ordered me to hire a private attorney just in case Carletha filed a civil law suit against the office. I asked him why I should do that since the office of the governor already had legal representation for his many cases pertaining to his office. But Adam and then interim general council Jesse Panuccio promised I would be reimbursed for any expenses. So I contracted with an attorney Adam recommended. When my monthly bills matched that of my take-home pay, I showed them to Adam and reminded him of his commitment to reimburse me. He flat out said the Governor had said no. The price tag for having that lawyer on retainer was over $25,000, with no repayment from the governor's office. And all because of some nonsense someone had made up.

There were plenty of ways the media could have looked into the story that would have shown it was ridiculous. For example, Carletha had made a statement about how my travel aide and I always had to have adjoining rooms. Now, had the press bothered to ask, they could have found out that the adjoining room was for my security officer, not my travel aide. Nor did anyone in the press ever stop to ask if such behavior was compatible with my character or to consider talking to my other current employees, or previous employees. No one asked, "How could this have happened in the office without someone else noticing?" I had two doors to my office. My chief of staff sat at one door and my executive secretary sat at the other. How could a compromising situation have occurred without one of them seeing something, or without my security officer seeing something, as he would have been with me at the time? These kinds of questions were never asked of Carletha, so she never had to account for the day and time that this incident supposedly occurred. Instead, the media saw sensationalism written all over the story and just ran with it without validating the credibility of the source or the accuracy of the allegations.

Here's the kicker: Carletha never made this claim while she worked for me. This information only came up eight months after she was fired, and only after she was brought up on felony charges. Gary Fineout just reported the story, without doing any homework.

The whole thing lasted for a while and the press continued to hound me about this invented incident. Yet they gave Carletha, the accuser, a pass. As a self-professed minister, Carletha should have followed Exodus 20: "Thou shalt not bear false witness against thy neighbor."

During the eight months after she was fired, Carletha told a mutual friend John Davis that she was mad at me for not preventing her from being fired. Carletha contacted a former House member, Scott Plakon, to encourage him to run against me as lieutenant governor. She started a Twitter account and Facebook page dedicated to impeaching the lieutenant governor, all the while never repeating the claim that she had made in her polygraph. When things like this happen, it can be hard to remember that freedom of the press and freedom of speech are two of the blessed things about America. But another great thing about our country is that the accused is innocent until proven guilty. Unfortunately, nowadays, when cases are tried in the press as much as in the courtroom, when the media is the judge, jury, and executioner, the accused are often guilty until proven innocent. And if they can prove they're innocent (they have to do the work, because the press will not), the news organizations might grant them a retraction that few people will ever hear or read about.

Since they're not the ones making up the stories but just reporting them, too many people in the media give themselves a pass. They hide behind their First Amendment protections. And in our current social media culture, the same old stories are just regurgitated, whether they're true or not. And the more sensational they are, the more regurgitation there is. It's not as if journalists don't realize this happens. Whatever happened to journalistic ethics?

What could I do in the face of all this? I felt the same way when the governor made it sound as if I had resigned because I was caught up in a scandal.

The stories get away from you and away from the truth so quickly. And once they're reported, they're out there forever. Whenever someone looks up my name, these stories are attached. Never mind that they're false stories. They're attached to me forever.

Back when I was in the military, I was accepted for a remote college degree program at Kensington University in California. This was 1987, so we didn't have the Internet, and remote schooling wasn't that common. But because I was working and often away on six-month deployments, it was the only way to get my graduate degree. I graduated from the program in 1989. At the time, the university was certified under the California code. But in 1994 an audit of the university was done by the California Bureau for Private Postsecondary and Vocational Education, after which, Kensington University lost its certification.

In 2003 a reporter was doing a story about degree mills, saw Kensington University on my resume, and decided to lump it with his story so he could include my name. He made it sound as if I hadn't completed all the coursework at Kensington but just purchased a degree from the school. The story didn't even specify Kensington as a degree mill, since the university received full approval to offer degrees from the Council for Private Postsecondary and Vocational Education in California since 1976, and then lost its certification in the late 1990s. The story went out, however, that I didn't get a real degree.

I called a local media station, and because I'd kept all of my records and still had my coursework, I brought them to the interview and took the local reporter through everything I'd done to earn my degree. I even showed him my grades. And he did write a story about it, but it ended up being a blip. When the truth comes out, it doesn't make the same waves.

In 2009 and 2010 Pam Bondi, the current attorney general, did not list checking account balances or income on her financial disclosures. Later when the press asked questions, she filed an amended financial disclosure correcting it. Pam's net worth increased 65 percent since taking office. This stories was barely a blip in the media. Back in 2009, I submitted my financial disclosure, and there was a comma in the wrong place. It looked as if I had $200 million in assets when it should have read $20 million. When I discovered the error, I made the correction and reported it accurately. That became a news story forever. Year after year, if my name came up in the press, they found a reason to include a mention of it.

The only difference between Pam and me is that I'm a member of a minority ethnicity and she's not. I firmly believe that being a black Republican made me a good punching bag. If I were a black Democrat, I would have had civil rights groups coming to my defense during some of these incidents. As a black Republican, there's really no support mechanism, no powerful contingent to back you up. We just don't have the numbers. We're really on the outskirts, even in our own party. And if you don't have a power group to back you up, the media can get away with malpractice.

It took me a while to realize how damaging these stories could be and how they would attach to me forever, every time someone did a Google search for my name. Today, when the press writes about me, they might throw in "never charged" or a one-liner such as, "She has not been accused of any wrongdoing," but only after they've rehashed the whole Allied Veterans affair. As a matter of fact, when the FDLE released its report reviewing criminal connections with Allied, the report stated, "Based upon information obtained pursuant to FDLE's investigation, Carroll's business relationship with Allied Veterans of the World and her subsequent actions do not appear to violate any criminal Florida Statute." Yet this exoneration of any criminal activity did not make the headlines or clear my name.

The governor has done real damage to my reputation, which could make it difficult for me to find meaningful employment or be considered for board service in the future, or even run for office again, not to mention what it's done to me personally, and my family—and for no reason. As I stated before, if Governor Scott had wanted me to leave, all he had to do was ask.

CHAPTER 10

MOVING ON

*"Trust in the Lord with all your heart
and lean not on your own understanding;
in all your ways submit to him, and
he will make your paths straight."*

—*Proverbs 3:5–6*

The governor didn't appoint another lieutenant governor for another ten months or so, which I think supports my belief that he never wanted one in the first place. He finally appointed someone only after the Legal of Women Voters brought a lawsuit against him because he was risking the line of succession by not having a lieutenant governor. If something happened to him—and we did have this happen to one of our governors who had a heart attack while riding an exercise bike—there wouldn't have been a next-in-line. The new lieutenant governor is being treated even worse than I was from what I hear. He only has a small staff and he doesn't have security. They gave him a car to drive himself around in. They haven't given him much to do. The state has 19 million people and it takes 10 hours or more to drive from one corner to the other. It has a population that's so diverse that no one person could truly represent it well.

I've written this book because I felt it was important to put the full truth out there and then put the whole thing behind me. Even in hard times, life is full of great lessons, and I've surely learned by now that you can't win over all of your critics. It's wasted energy to try. I've also learned that you can't keep defending yourself forever. You could repeat yourself until the end of time and still not convince everyone. But that doesn't mean that the truth isn't important. It just means that I can't spend the rest of my days trying to get it heard.

I've also learned that eagles climb higher than crows. Rising above the criticism and not being distracted from the work that God has planned for me is what's before me now.

I still believe in giving people the benefit of the doubt and I believe that most people are worth supporting. If you start thinking that people are bad or they don't care or they're out to get you, it can end up poisoning you.

I recognize that saying, "Trust in your faith and believe in God because all the forces of darkness cannot keep you from where God wants you to go," is easier said than done. If a person doesn't have a strong religious foundation and family support as I have, then hardships can sometimes feel like too much to bear. That's when we have to really get deep into our souls and figure out who we are and what we want to do. We also have to remember that difficulties help us grow in patience and endurance, and they make our characters stronger. In everyone's life rain will fall. Sometimes it comes in the form of a monsoon, but we should know that it will stop and the sun will come out, with the grace of God. The greater the battle, the greater the victory. God puts pressure on you so that he can move his spirit into you.

If there's one thing I hope people will take from this book, it's that it's possible to come out on the other side of anything and live another day. If you cannot do it by yourself, you need to get help, but it's still possible, no matter how harsh your reality. The truth is, not everyone is going to like you, but you can still live a good, kind, respectful life. Not everyone is going to treat you well, but you can still treat people with kindness and respect and treat yourself that way, too. Your future is too big to be distracted by obstacles. The more success you have, the more opportunities there will be for distractions. Someone once said, life is like photography, we develop from the negatives.

Not everything in life is going to work out, but you can still love yourself and know that you were born with innate abilities that allow you to contribute to this world in a multitude of ways, even if it's something as small as smiling at someone on a particular day when that person needed it most. You never know when the smallest thing you do will have a big impact on someone's life.

One of my regrets in all of this is that I'm a strong, independent person, for the most part, but I gave up some of that to be a team player and I abandoned my core. I struggled with my independence when I was growing up because I had such protective parents. I gained that independence by joining the military, but after getting into politics, I lost some of it for a while. I've admired people I've met along the way who have not wavered on their independence and spoke their minds despite all the pressure not to. If I had to do it all over again, I would be a whole lot more prepared for dealing with the media and dealing with the people who use the media to further their agenda. I would also be a whole lot more prepared to stand up for myself and make really clear what I would not accept. Not defending myself was my fault, another of life's lessons learned.

At the end of the day, working for the people of Florida was a privilege. Perhaps it's true that no good deed goes unpunished, but I still believe in doing good deeds. My advice is to do your best and be your best in each moment.

When you get there, wherever there may be, take time to enjoy your accomplishments. When you get there smell the roses and give thanks to God for bringing you through that journey. When you get there learn to give back; service above self is the greatest gift you can give. In giving freely, you fruitfully receive. In teaching you truly learn. Not everyone will go through your journey, but lessons learned can be shared to help others achieve higher heights. Sometimes the journey will be tough, but know that you succeeded because you have the power within you to do so. I wrote this book to remind myself, and hopefully others, that bad news is never the final chapter.

ABOUT THE AUTHOR

J ennifer Sandra Carroll was born in Port of Spain, Trinidad West Indies, and immigrated to the United States as a young child. She enlisted in the United States Navy in 1979 rising from the ranks of an enlisted jet mechanic E-1 to retire as a Lieutenant Commander, Aviation Maintenance Officer after 20 years. During her time in the Navy she served during Desert Storm and Desert Shield and was awarded numerous awards that include: Meritorious Service Medal, two Navy Commendation Medals, two Navy Achievement Medals, two Joint Meritorious Unit Award, three Meritorious Unit Commendation Ribbons, U.S. Coast Guard Operations Ribbon, Navy "E", Good Conduct Ribbon, National Defense Service Medal, two Navy Volunteer Service Medal, two Sea Service Ribbons,

Overseas Ribbon, Navy Recruiting Service Ribbon, two Coast Guard Special Operations Service Ribbons, and an Expert Pistol Medal.

Jennifer was the President of Carroll & Carroll Consulting and company renamed to 3N.&J.C. Corp., from and the Owner of Great Clips Franchises.

President George W. Bush appointed Jennifer to the White House Presidential Scholar's Commission, and the Veterans' Disability Benefits Commission.

As a legislator, Jennifer worked to pass meaningful legislation that enhanced economic development, which included: procuring $2.9 million to fund the Florida Export Finance Corporation to help employers have access to short term loans in order to retain and create jobs. She sponsored the Entertainment Economic Development Legislation that created thousands of jobs for Floridians who were paid over $485 million in wages. Jennifer helped obtain $10 million to support Florida Community College of Jacksonville's Aircraft Coating Educational Facility located at Cecil Field. She was successful in securing $2 million dollars statewide for the Boy Scouts Learning for Life program and $700,000 for the Girl Scouts character education functions. Jennifer also passed a domestic violence legislation that made shelters more secure by giving law enforcement authority to arrest and significantly increase penalties for anyone trespassing at a domestic violence shelter.

Jennifer served as Deputy Majority Leader, Majority Whip, Vice Chairwoman of the Transportation and Economic Development Appropriations Committee, Chairwoman of the

Finance Committee, Chairwoman of the Economic Development Policy Council, Chairwoman of the Financial Institutions Committee, Vice-Chair of the Ethics and Elections Committee; served on the: Homeland Security & Public Safety Committee, Energy & Utilities Policy Committee, Economic Development & Community Affairs Policy Council, Select Policy Council on Strategic & Economic Planning and Jobs & Entrepreneurship Council, Finance & Tax, Growth Management and Business Regulation Committees.

Jennifer was the former Executive Director of Florida Department of Veterans' Affairs. She was responsible for the claims and benefits of over 1.8 million veterans. Under her leadership, more than $63 million in retroactive compensation was awarded to Florida's veterans. She lobbied for the retention of state construction funds for the Bay and Charlotte County State Veterans' Nursing Homes, and led the generation of two federal matching grant applications that resulted in $15 million of federal funds for these projects. She was also the Chairperson for Florida's Council on Homelessness. Jennifer sought ways for Florida to provide enhanced services toward solving homeless problems in the state, particularly within the veteran's community. She also worked closely with the Department of Veterans' Affairs to secure Jacksonville as a site to receive a national veteran's cemetery.

In addition to her duties assisting the Governor with economic development and foreign trade, as Lieutenant Governor Jennifer oversaw the Florida Department of Military Affairs, Florida Department of Veterans Affairs, and was Chairperson of Space Florida. She was also the Governor's Designee on the Florida Defense Support Task Force, and Chairperson on the Governor's Task Force on Citizen Safety and Protection. She traveled to Washington, D.C. to meet with Congressional and Pentagon officials to advocate for Florida's $65 billion military economy and defense industry. Jennifer's efforts resulted in increased military positions, military construction funding and increased defense contract opportunities for Florida's businesses. Jennifer was particularly active in protecting Florida's military installations from encroachment and has helped move several projects that not only stop development near military activities but protects and conserves Florida's precious natural lands and waterways. Jennifer led trade missions to South Africa, and Trinidad and Tobago that led to $40 million in new trade between Florida and South Africa and yielded $30 million in trade between Trinidad and Tobago and Florida. Her work as Chairwoman of Space Florida was instrumental in creating thousands of new private sector, space and aerospace related jobs in Florida.

Jennifer was invited by the United States Department of State's Bureau of International Information Programs to lecture on the U.S. presidential election process.

Jennifer was recognized by VWise for her efforts igniting veteran women in business. Awards received: Rotary Club of Orange Park Citizen of the Year Award, World Trade Center Miami - International Women's Day Award for promotion of free trade and international business in the Americas, Boy Scouts of America - Twelve Points Award for her service to youth and the community, The Grio Top 100 People Making History Today - Class of 2012, and the Distinguished African American Woman of Florida Award - The James Weldon Johnson Branch Association for the Study of African American Life and History.

Education: St. Leo University, masters of business administration, 2008; University of New Mexico, bachelors of arts in political science, 1985. Honorary Degree, Doctor of Laws - Saint Leo University and Associate in Science, Honoris Cusa - Miami Dade College.

Jennifer is married to Nolan Carroll of Miami Florida for 31 years and they have three accomplished children, Nolan II, Nyckie and Necho.

CPSIA information can be obtained at www.ICGtesting.com
Printed in the USA
LVOW10s2210111114

413231LV00012B/274/P

2439052